BY CHARLES BUKOWSKI

CHARLES BUKOWSKI

DANGLING IN THE TOURNEFORTIA

BLACK SPARROW PRESS - SANTA ROSA - 1992

ACKNOWLEDGMENT

Grateful acknowledgment is given to the following magazines where
some of these poems originally appeared: *Alcatraz, American Poetry Review, Bachy, Barney, The Berkeley Poetry Review, Cedar
Rock, Fireweed, New York Quarterly, Poetry L.A., Poetry Now, Scree,
The Spirit that Moves Us, Tendril, Winners,* and *Wormwood Review.*

LIBRARY OF CONGRESS CATALOGING IN PUBLICATION DATA

Bukowski, Charles.
    Dangling in the tournefortia.
    I. Title.
PS3552.U4D27   811'.54   81-10145
ISBN 0-87685-526-5   AACR2
ISBN 0-87685-525-7 (pbk.)

Sixth Printing

To John Fante

The tournefortia is a large tropical tree, ideally suited to the Southern California climate, that produces small delicate flowers and a kind of fleshy fruit.

TABLE OF CONTENTS

Dangling in the Tournefortia

the lady in red

people went into vacant lots and pulled up greens to cook and the
men rolled Bull Durham or smoked Wings (10¢ a pack) and the
dogs were thin and the cats were thin and the cats learned how to
catch mice and rats and the dogs caught and killed the cats (some
of the cats), and gophers tore up the earth and people killed them
by attaching garden hoses to the exhaust pipes of their cars and
sticking the hoses into the gopher holes and when the gophers
came out the cats and the dogs and the people were afraid of
them, they circled and showed their long thin teeth, then they
stopped and shivered and as they did the cats rushed in followed
by the dogs. people raised chickens in their back yards and the
roosters were weak and the hens were thin and the people ate
them if they didn't lay eggs fast enough, and the best time of all
was when John Dillinger escaped from jail, and one of the
saddest times of all was when the Lady in Red fingered him and
he was gunned down coming out of that movie.
Pretty Boy Floyd, Baby Face Nelson, Machine Gun Kelly, Ma
Barker, Alvin Karpis, we loved them all. and there were always
wars starting in China and they never lasted long but the
newspapers had big black headlines: WAR IN CHINA!
the '30s were a time when people had very little and there was
nothing to hide behind, and that Bull Durham tag dangling from
the string coming out of your pocket—that showed you had it,
you could roll with one hand—plenty of time to practice and if
somebody looked at you wrong or said something you didn't
like you cracked him one right in the mouth. it was a glorious
non-bullshit time, especially after we got rid of Herbert Hoover.

13

the stink

when I was eleven or twelve one summer I used to hitchhike 20
miles to the beach and look at the water and the sand, it was
all much cleaner then and every day this fat woman would
drag her dog by on a leash pulling him through the water as
she walked along
the dog was big and wet and beaten and cowed and the fat
woman smelled of whiskey
the wind brought it to me
and I don't think the sea gulls liked it
and I hated that woman and her whiskey smell
and what she did to that dog
I would have killed her if I could
she was so terribly fat
she was bunches of fat hanging out of her
bathing suit
and the whiskey smell
and the terrified dog.
I couldn't understand what was wrong with her or why she
did it
why she needed whiskey.
there was nothing in my life as ugly as she was.

now I have been drunk for 40 years and I hear all the
voices of those I have known as one voice:
"you just aren't yourself when you get drunk, you are
one of the meanest drunks I have ever seen, you are
disgusting. . ."

well, I don't ask them to hang around and they don't.

the lisp

I had her for 3 units
and at mid-term
she'd read off how many assignments
stories
had been turned in:
"Gilbert: 2. . .
Ginsing: 5. . .
McNulty: 4. . .
Frijoles: none. . .
Lansford: 2. . .
Bukowski: 38. . ."

the class laughed
and she lisped
that not only did Bukowski
write many stories
but that they were all of
high quality.

she flashed her golden legs
in 1940 and there was something
sexy about her lisp
sexy as a hornet
as a rattler
that lisp.

and she lisped to me
after class
that I should go to
war,
that I would make a

very good sailor,
and she told me about how
she took my stories home
and read them to her husband
and how they both laughed,
and I told her, "o.k., Mrs. Anderson."
and I'd walk out on the campus
where almost every guy had a
girl.

I didn't become a sailor,
Mrs. Anderson, I'm not crazy
about the ocean
and I didn't like war
even when it was the popular
thing to
do.

but here's another completed assignment
for you
those golden legs
that lisp
still has me typing
love songs.

silk

silken kneecaps
blue garters
pink garters
all through the depression
better than the
N.R.A.
the W.P.A.
silken legs for
Cagney and Gable and
all the boys in the neighborhood.

now that pantyhose is worn
a man no longer gets to watch
a strange woman on the streets
with her fine legs
pulling her stockings up
stretching that silk over the
kneecaps
with just a glimpse of white flesh
and pink petticoat. . .
I suppose it's best, though, that
women be comfortable.
I wouldn't like to go around pulling
my stockings up
continually, yet
some of us who remember
are still wistful about that era
dreaming of those legs of the
1930s

legs no longer beautiful now

or legs that are dead
simply bone
but legs we remember the other
way
those legs that kept the silkworms
busy
legs that were for our fathers
our uncles
legs for Cagney and Gable and
all the boys in the neighborhood.

on shooting

I think I'd like to put one
bullet
just in front of one of the rear legs
of one of those big grey wrinkled
elephants

and I'd like to be on the roof
and put one shot into the Goodyear
blimp

as a boy I never got to do
the things I wanted to do
like peek under the dress of
the lady next door
without her knowing I was
doing it

I'd get to see all the way up her
legs
to the panties
and they'd be
pink.

I'd like to shoot an
alligator
right below the eye
and see him whirl the
waters muddy.

I'd like to put a bullet into
a church steeple

even though I'm neither a believer nor
a disbeliever

I'd like to stand on a high ledge
and rip 8 or ten shots into the
Pacific Ocean.

if the lady next door had only
let me look up her legs *without*
her knowing it

I remember her name:
Mabel
and she'd talk to me
and her face was full of sexy
wrinkles and sadness
her eyes were tiny shots of
blue water
deathly and bland
but her legs were magic and
teasing
double pillars of maddening
thou-shalt-not-have
in high black pumps and nylon
with her cost accountant husband
getting it
all.

she knew what I
wanted
her tiny smile
told me.

Mabel, you
whore.

blue collar solitude

picking up two six-packs
after work
to hell with dinner
going to the apartment
and stripping down
to your shorts
throwing your clothes
on the floor
climbing onto the bed
no shower
no bath
sitting up against
the pillow
and cracking open
the first tall beer can
lighting a cigarette
nothing to do
nobody to talk to
looking at the wallpaper
yesterday's dishes
stacked in the sink
look out the window
the room getting darker
open the second can
of beer
no wife
no tv
no children

sitting in your
underwear

drinking beer
alone

everything's gone
the foreman
the time clock
the grocery store clerks
the newspaper
the coffee shops

the phone rings
you listen
and listen and
listen

until it stops

another beer

hearing the breath
whistle up your
nostrils

wiggling the right
toe

watching
it.

sick

I had this night job and I'd sit in bed
looking out the window in the late afternoon
the last of the sun filtering into the room
through the leaves and branches of a large green bush
and when I thought about what was out there
waiting, I'd reach for the telephone.
the office clerk knew my voice:
"yes, Bukowski, what is it this time?"
"just write something down," I'd tell him,
"common cold, flu, the clap. . ."
I'd hang up.
it was good watching it slowly get dark
listening to people coming home
parking their cars, turning on their tv's
making kitchen sounds, talking.

then I'd get up and drink for three or four hours
alone,
then go back to bed and sleep.

and the next night at the factory everybody
would seem very small and wrinkled
and I'd walk in tall and shining
eyes calm and cool
secretly assured;
the men didn't understand and the girls
all loved me, and the foreman would come forward
to speak to me of absenteeism
as I took out a cigarette, lit it and
listened.

immortals

the old jazz place
                in the French Quarter
New Orleans
                those great names
they went back decades
                        but they were tired
those old blacks
                they were tired and old
but they still had style
they pumped it out
it was authentic
                they pumped it out
and they
        were drinking too like
the rest of us
and in between sets
we all used the same broken toilet to
piss in
        and they stood there
hitting on joints
                getting ready to
do it again
        for 25 or 30 more tourists
the all-white audience.
they were great and they were tired
and they were
                overweight
most of them
                bald
now almost all of them are dead

and I don't recall the jazz
                    so much
anymore
          only that we all pissed
in the same broken toilet
between sets
              their sets.

Independence Day

it was the 4th of July and I was
living with an Alvarado Street whore,
I was on my last unemployment check
and we had a room on the first floor
of a Beacon Street hotel next to a
housing development.
it was 11 a.m. and I was puking,
trying to get a can of ale down,
the whore in bed next to me
in her torn slip
mumbling about her children in
Atlanta
then sleeping, snoring
her belly like a watermelon
fattening with green beer and red
wine,
she was the best I could do,
on and off with her
for two years—
then two kids came up and
threw a firecracker
FLANNNNGGGG!
against the screen of our
window.
"oooh shit," said the whore.
I got up out of bed
in my torn shorts: "hey, you
fuckers! don't do that again!"
they laughed and ran off.
"I miss my children," said the
whore, "I wonder if I'll ever

see Ronnie and Lila again?"
"will you stop that shit?"
I asked. "I heard that shit
all last night long!"
the whore began crying.
I went to the bathroom and
puked again,
cracked a new can of ale and
sat next to the whore
in my bed.
"don't mourn, Lilly," I said,
"you give a great blowjob and
that counts for something."
FLANNNNGGGG!
it was another firecracker.
"ooh shit," said the whore.
I leaped up and ran to the
window.
I was 25 years old and a mean
s.o.b.
I had nothing to lose and was
willing to
lay it down anywhere.
"I *told* you fuckers!
that's *all*!
that's the end of it!
the next time will be the
last time!"
they just stood there and
laughed at me, two little kids
maybe ten or eleven years old,
they laughed at me,
me who duked it out
once or twice a week
with the most violent characters

in the neighborhood,
maybe not always winning
but hardly ever shamed.
one of the kids lit another cracker
and tossed it,
FLANNNNGGGG!
I opened the screen and leaped
through the window
into the yard.
the kids backed off.
"go get your father," I said,
and I'll kick his ass good!"
they stood looking at me.
"fucking drunk," said the
tallest kid and he pulled out
a switchblade, hit the button,
the knife flicked out and he
jammed it into a tree, then
pulled it out.
I moved toward him and
he stood there
making movements with the
blade.
I closed in on him,
he flicked out, ran a gash
along my right arm
above the wrist
and then I had the knife
twisted it away from him
and kicked him in the ass.
"now get your father,"
I said.
they both left
and I stood there waiting
in my torn shorts. . .

a minute, two minutes,
three minutes,
then I got afraid the heat
might arrive
so I went back and
crawled into the window,
got back in the bed
and played with the knife,
flicking the blade
in and out.
I took a hit of ale
and didn't puke.
I felt masterful—nobody
could have handled it better—
I was one 25-year-old
mean rattlesnake bastard,
it didn't pay to fuck with
me.
"ooh, you're bleeding,"
noticed the whore.
"I'm having my period,"
I told her.
"I always thought you were
a queer," she said.
"I never knew queers had
periods."

it was a beautiful knife,
I sat there flicking it in
and out.
I opened a new ale.
I never liked holidays.
this one was no
exception.

"I miss my kids,"
said the whore,
"you don't know how much
I miss my kids. . ."
her watermelon gut
moved up and down
under her torn and dirty slip.

I had about half a can
of ale left
and I lifted it
and I poured it
over the top of her
head
and it ran
down over her hair
and down her face
and into her nostrils
and over her lips
and she sat up
angrily:
"why, you *cheap* queer
bastard!"

"baby," I smiled at her,
"go easy, I am one tough
son of a bitch. . ."

one for Sherwood Anderson

sometimes I forget about him and his peculiar
innocence, almost idiotic, awkward and mawkish,
he liked walking over bridges and through cornfields.
tonight I think about him, the way the lines were,
one felt space between his lines, air
and he told it so the lines remained
carved there
something like Van Gogh.
he took his time
looking about
sometimes running to save something
leaving everything to save something,
then at other times giving it all away.
he didn't understand Hemingway's neon tattoo,
found Faulkner much too clever.
he was a midwestern hick
he took his time.
he was as far away from Fitzgerald as he was
from Paris.
he told stories and left the meaning open
and sometimes he told meaningless stories
because that was the way it was.
he told the same story again and again
and he never wrote a story that was unreadable.
and nobody ever talks about his life or
his death.

fight on

pretty boy was tiring
punching against useless junk
his arms were weary
and the wino closed in and
it became ugly
pretty boy dropped his hands
and the wino had him by the
throat
banging his head hard against the
wall of the building.
pretty boy fell
the wino paused
then landed several kicks
in the genital area
turned and walked back through
the dark end of the alley
toward some of us.
we parted to let him
through
and he walked past us
turned
looked back
lit a cigarette
and then moved on.

when I got back in
she was raging:
"where the hell you been?"
pink-eyed she was
sitting up against the pillows
her slippers on.

"stop for another *quickie*?
no wonder you haven't
had it up for a week!"

"I saw a good one. free.
better than anything at the
Olympic. I saw a good ass-
kicking alley fight."

"you expect me to believe
that?"

"Christ, don't you ever wash
any glasses? well, we'll use
these two."

I poured two. she knocked hers
off. well, she needed it
and I needed mine.

"it was really brutal. I hate
to see such things but I can't
stop watching."

"pour another drink."
I poured two more. she needed
hers because she lived with me.
I needed mine because I worked
as a stockroom boy
at the May Co.

"you stopped for a *quickie*!"

"no, I watched this fight."

she knocked her second drink
off. she was trying to decide
whether I had had a quickie or
whether I had watched a fight.

"pour us another drink. is that
the only bottle you've got?"

I winked at her and pulled
another bottle from the sack.
we seldom ate. we drank and
we drank and I worked as a
stockroom boy at the May Co.
and she had a pair of the
most beautiful legs I had
ever seen.

as I poured the third drink
she got up, kicked off her
slippers and put her high
heels on.

"we need some god damned
ice," she said and I watched
her as she walked toward the
kitchen.
then she vanished in there
and I thought about the
fight again.

I didn't want to

I was always a bad typist and I never learned to spell
because I didn't want to.

I never learned properly how to drive an automobile and I
   bought
my first one off a used car lot for $35, got in with
my drunken lady and almost ripped off the side of a
hospital making my first left turn.

I didn't want to learn music because I disliked
the teacher with her white wig and her powdered face.

I got stuck in the ROTC because I didn't want to be an
athlete and they put me in a manual of arms competition
and I didn't want to win and I won and they gave me a
medal and I threw it down a sewer.

I didn't learn music and now I listen to
more classical music than the first hundred people you'll
pass on the street.

I disdained money and my first wife was a millionairess.
she got rid of me and I never had any more wives.

I hated poets and I hated poetry and I began to write
poetry.
and one day I looked up and I was in Hamburg, Germany,
translated into a half dozen languages and there were
over a thousand people sitting in the seats and aisles,
perched on the rafters.
I read to them and they believed it.

ıdn't want to read books but I tried to read great poets and
ıovelists, men who have inspired thousands of people
throughout the centuries and the books fell from my hands
and I slept.

I went to museums of art and looked at the great
paintings and I was bored.
I didn't worry about it, I don't consider myself inadequate,
I consider them inadequate.

it is difficult for me to get interested or angry.
when a cop stops me for some infraction I simply sink
into some great sea of disgust.
"do you want to know what you did, sir?" he asks me.
"no," I say.

I have the same trouble with women.
"look, you just sit and don't say anything,"
they say. "now something is wrong if you just sit there
and don't say anything!"
I drain my drink and pour another.
"look," they say, "let's talk! let's work things
out!"
"I don't want to work things out," I tell them.

I don't even want to write and when I write
oft times a strange word will slip in and I'll leave
it in or I'll make a typing error, say I will mean to hit a
"g" and I'll hit an "h" and if it happens at the beginning
of a word then I'll use a word beginning with "h."
it doesn't matter.

even as a horseplayer I sometimes don't care.
once I was driving to Mexico from L.A. to go to
Caliente racetrack and ¾'s of the way down something

grabbed at the wheel and I turned right, down a street, and
parked near a railing overlooking a cliff. I got out of
the car and sat at the top of this cliff.
the ocean was 40 to 60 yards straight down and I had never been
charmed by the ocean but I sat there because
I just didn't want to go to the racetrack anymore.
I had no thoughts at all, I sat there feeling neither good
nor bad.
after some time I noticed three squirrels
climbing straight up the cliff toward me.
they came closer and closer, they bounded six inches or so at a
time, stopped, looked at me, then bounded closer.
they got unbelievably close, the three of them and their eyes
were beautiful, never had I seen eyes like that, never
on a woman, there was no treachery there, and men's eyes never
        interested me.
then, all at once, they ran off, bounding straight down the side of
the cliff, rapidly, sure-footed, without falling into the
ocean, and I became conscious of myself as a man, and worse,
as a writer, and I thought, I'll never be able to write this down.

I really did buy my first automobile for $35 and I asked the man,
"does the motor start? does it have a key?"
it didn't have any springs or a reverse gear and to make the
headlights work I'd have to hit a hard bump in the road,
and I had to park it on a hill to get it started,
it ran for two years without my changing the oil and when the
        car
finally died I just left it and walked away. the
drunken lady who had been along for that first ride past the
hospital, she lived a little longer, with me and without me,
but mostly with me, she died and I buried her one warm
afternoon north of Anaheim, and the best thing I liked about
her was she never said, "let's talk this thing out."
she was a typist for a large downtown furniture store

and she had the most beautiful legs I have ever seen before or
since.

I should have loved her more than I did but I didn't want
to.

nothing

when I was in
the post office
there was a
black girl

there was something
wrong
with her
and
there was something
wrong
with me

one
lunch period
she
walked up to me
and said,
"come on, buy
me a drink."

so
we walked
across the street
to the
Chinaman's
and we
had the drink
and
then I said,
"come on, buy
me a drink."

and
she did
and then we
noticed a guy
passed out in a
corner booth
and she said,
"Jesus Christ,
it's
Skinny Minny!"

Skinny Minny was
a high yellow
supervisor who had
given me
plenty of trouble

and it
looked strange
to see him there
human enough
to get drunk
like that

"I don't hate
him
so much
now," I
told her.

we finished
our drinks
and walked out
to go back to
work

"come on over here," she
said

and she led me
up a little alley
to a wire
fence
where some
empty cartons
were stacked

it was very
dark and
she pulled over
a carton
sat down and
unzipped me
and began licking me
and then she
had me
in her mouth
sucking

I grabbed the
wire fence
"JESUS, JESUS,
JESUS!"

I came

she zipped me
up
and we walked
back to work
and punched in

late

*

after that
night
we never went
out together
again

maybe she had
been
playing me
against
some other guy

but Skinny Minny
never looked
as bad
again

I don't know
what
that night
meant
it probably
didn't mean
anything
at all

it's when you
look
for meaning
that you get
confused

about a month
later
she said goodby
and quit
the job

that
made sense.

taking care of the big whammy

I forget which year it was
but as so happens
every now and then
a war between the U.S.A.
and somebody somewhere else
was getting closer.

I guess if we had not been so
tired from working overtime and
had read our newspapers more carefully
we might have known about it.

one night my supervisor handed me
a piece of paper
and I thought it was just another
write-up
as I stuck it into my pocket
and kept jamming letters into the
case before me.

but my buddy, Miles, to my left
said, "hey, Hank, better read
this one. tonight we all got one."

I took it out and read it.
it talked about possible
hydrogen bomb warfare.

first, they told us that
we were just as important as the
navy, the marines, the army

and that in case
all was melted into
vapor
we would still continue to draw
our paychecks if
under code 809 we
went to area 773 and
declared 662. that
was it.

but what I liked best was
that on our coffee break
one hour and 30 minutes after
being told
where we could still
draw our pay even after everything was
turned into a flaming ball
of shit

none of us
talked about that.
we talked only about whether
the Dodgers would hold onto
their half-game lead
through September and whether
the new supervisor with the
great legs would turn out
to be a
bitch or a bastard.

she turned out to be
both. the Dodgers didn't
hold and we kept getting our
paychecks at the same old
place.

the government had lost its
cool
printing that pamphlet
and
in hidden places
we talked and laughed about it
a little.

Russia, we said, they were talking
about Russia.

and a big black guy
pounding on a candy machine that
had robbed him of a dime
yelled,
"well, I say: let's BOMB those
fuckers BEFORE they bomb us!"

we all let out a big cheer
then walked back to our cases
and began jamming
letters
again.

the Indian

the old Indian in Texas
was a handyman in return for
some beans and a shack and some
money for wine.
he didn't want much.
he didn't do much.
I knew the rich people who had
hired him: I had married their
granddaughter.
she had everything and wanted
more.
she wore high–heels and
crunched the earth when she
walked. it jolted her
frame.
her hair bounced like a horse's mane
as she went about.
she told me the Indian's name
and I saw him mending fences sometimes
a long tan rolled cigarette
hanging from his mouth
and at the most curious
times
a tiny blue puff of smoke
emanated from it.
I liked his face
it had diggings, veins, rivers, burnt areas.
he was never in a hurry.
I wasn't either
his back looked like it was tied
to a pine board

while I was bent and slumped
weary and with
gut.

there wasn't much to do on that ranch
for either of us.
I took long walks while my wife
painted oil paintings. she
painted best alone and I respected
that.
I came back each evening with
dust on my
shoes.

in time
in not too long a time
the Indian began to die. he knew
the landscape.
he didn't want the hospital. he
wanted to die in his shack, he
told them.

they obliged.
he died there
secure
untroubled
and easy.
he wanted to die
there
and he did
with his cigarettes and wine jug.

my wife went on painting
and grandmother went on with her
migraines

and grandfather played old cowboy
songs on the victrola;
listening with a drink in his hand
he asked me,
"you like that one, Hank?"

"yeah, I think it's good,"
I told him.

grace

the lady is passing with the tray
throw an apple into the sky
hit the bluebird
let the buildings fall
pay your phone bill
and let the Virgins die
waiting for your sword.

such seething in the orchards.
the people want your act
ordained
perpetuated like
the stink of the Mediterranean

as the tired trains crawl
Europe
I walk out on this balcony
as the sky
explodes your name.

get your phone bill and
burn your mail, Manolete,
you were one of those
who made people not
tired of death, you
tried like that.

love and courage

the one I liked was where Cagney
fought in the ring
got punchy
so he could earn money
to give his brother
music lessons—
the brother wanted to be a
classical pianist
was said to have
great talent
but they both came from the Lower
East Side, and
so Cagney got into the ring
again and again
for money to help the talented brother
become a classical pianist.
Cagney even loses the girl—
to his brother
and it ends with his brother
making it
(at Carnegie Hall, if I remember)
and Cagney
punched-out and blind
at his newsstand
listening to the radio
to his brother in the concert
hall,
and, of course, the girl is at the
hall
adoring, wild-eyed
as Cagney warms his hands over a
small fire

alone in the cold
he listens to the radio
as his brother plays
the piano,
Cagney
not knowing shit about music
and
hearing the final applause
believes that
all the beatings he has taken
were worthwhile.

two drunks

I was trying to write.
I was barely existing.
mostly I typed dirty things
for the girly magazines.

Eddie was trying to paint.
he was barely existing
but he was luckier than
I: he lived in this big
house
with this beautiful girl
who was
taking care of him.

Eddie and I were
drinking together.
we did our work
plenty of it but we
drank plenty too.

he had
all his paintings
down in the cellar
of this house—
hundreds of them
thrown about and
stuck together.

he painted only with
yellow paint run through
with black india ink.

yellow was
my favorite color so
I liked the paintings.

I stayed over there
in the daytime
and drank
and then at night I
went back to my place
and drank some more
and typed.

it was
an exciting time even
though
we were hardly
making it
and the madhouse and/
or skid row were just
around the corner.

we fought and screamed and
drank with strangers
and the sun was always
up or
it was midnight
and either way
it was
raw shit energy.

Eddie liked to
paint to music
and since that was the
way I wrote I
understood it.

"read me some of your
god damned poems. . ."

I'd read them and
he'd begin
violently ripping
the canvas
with his brush
black across yellow
his beautiful woman watching.

we must have
gone on like that for
two or three months.

one day
I went over
to see Eddie and
his girl
met me
at the door.

"Eddie's gone," she
said, "I kicked his
ass out!"

"did he take his paintings?"

"no, I trashed
them!"

she didn't look
beautiful to me
anymore.

"do you know
where he went?"

"no, and I don't
give a damn!"

she
closed the door.

Eddie never came by
my place.
every now and then I'd
wonder about him.

I even got drunk
one night and went
back to the house and
tried to make
his x-girlfriend.

I couldn't do it.
I went back home.

I had to keep
typing.
I was 50 years old
and
didn't have a job.

I even tried to
paint
but I was
no way near
as good as Eddie.

I went back to
writing dirty stories.

I never saw
Eddie again.
and after a while
I just
forgot about him

until tonight
ten years later.

Eddie, I don't care
much for people

but you could have
come by
you could have slept on the couch
or the floor.

not much
I know

but yellow is
my favorite color

just in case
you see this poem.

bad press

years ago while I was living on DeLongpre Ave.
typing at that window facing the sidewalk
he came by
a college professor
he came by with beer and I drank most of the
beer.
I don't remember much about the conversation
but I do remember that I wasn't very excited
by his visit.

one afternoon he came by and I had the flu.

I met him at the door. "I can't see you,"
I told him.

then I took the 6-pack he was holding from
him and closed the door leaving him
standing there.

many years later now I receive literary magazines
to which I don't subscribe.

and in them are reviews by this professor of
the anthologies I am in.
the professor always praises many, damns
a few, and when it comes to me he simply
blows me off the page like
cigarette ash that has fallen there.

I really *had* the flu, you know.
it didn't kill me but it certainly did appear
to ravage my talents.

yeah, man?

the court was going to hell
all these little
light brown guys
moved in

they parked on the front lawn
where he used to park alone
and they had him blocked in
with these old cars,
smashed giant battleships of
cars.

there was one little brown guy who
had his car on blocks
he had all four wheels off
the car had one headlight
missing and the bumper was
dragging.
the guy was in dungarees
and an undershirt
leaning against his fender
smoking a cigarette.

Larry walked out there.
he walked up to the guy
leaning up against the
fender.

"hey, man, you're blockin'
me in!" Larry told him.

the guy didn't say anything.
he just kept leaning there
smoking his cigarette.

"I want to get my car out
and yours is in the way!"
Larry told him.

the guy exhaled. "yeah,
man?" he just kept leaning
against the fender.

Larry went back into his
room.
he could see the guy
leaning there.
Larry began to drink Scotch
with beer chasers.

the more he thought about it
the more violated
he felt.

Larry kept drinking and
looking out the window
at the guy
and the guy just stayed
there
like that
for 30 minutes
for an hour.

suddenly Larry screamed,
"GOD DAMN SHIT!"
and he went to the bedroom

and got his big blade
and ran out
slamming the door

then he walked up
to the guy
slowly
and stopped.
Larry had most of
the blade
palmed in his hand
and he covered the
length of it
with a finger
and then he pushed
the tip of it into
the guy's undershirt
and said,
"move your car."

and the guy said,
"sure, man, all you had
to do was tell me."

then the guy
went to his place
and came back with
3 other little brown
guys
and they started putting
the wheels back
on the car.
they were fast.
but starting the car
was another matter.

Larry went back into his
room
and stood in the window
where they could
see him
drinking and
watching them

they finally got the car
started and the first guy
got in and
drove it off.

Larry came out
got into his car
and drove off slowly
for some six-packs
and some
fried chicken.

he got the stuff
came back
and noticed that his
front door was
unlocked
it was half open
and when he walked
in
his walls were
spray painted with
sloppy designs and
words
he couldn't
understand.

his radio was gone
he didn't have a tv
but his electric clock
was gone
all the pillows were
gone
the sheets
the dresser drawers
were scattered
the mattress was
slashed and
the stuffing
pulled out.

all the faucets were
running.
they had pissed on the
kitchen floor
broken eggs on it
dumped his garbage
there.

all his knives, forks and spoons were
gone
the salt and pepper were gone
the bread and coffee were gone
everything in the refrigerator was
gone

and in the bathroom
the toilet paper was gone
and the mirror broken
the cabinet emptied
razor
shaving cream

toothpaste
band–aids
aspirins
everything
gone.

and then he looked
in the toilet
and down in the bowl
was a freshly-cut
cat's tail
furry and still
bleeding
in the water

Larry hit the lever
to flush it away
but got an
empty click
lifted the lid
looked inside
and all
the toilet parts
were gone.

he walked into the
front room
sat on the couch
that was
without cushions
reached down
into the brown bag
pulled out a beer
cracked it open and
had a good hit.

he decided then
that it was about time
he moved
further west.

ladies' man

there were knocks at my door at 3 or 4 a.m.

my getting up to let in some drunk and crazy
woman

that always charmed me somehow, even though
those women were drugged or drunk and had
little feeling for me

it was low-level action, going to the refrigerator for beer, drinking with them until
5 or 6 a.m.

then going to bed with them those vicious
children of the night

I hated daylight and to be awakened by them
at noon as they stood before the mirror
putting on their monstrously red mouths:
"hey, can I use your phone?"

they came and they left and they came
again

the mailman used to see some of them
leaving

he watched those buttocks swing down the
lane

those high heels crashing through the sunlight flooding
the cement

"Jesus, man," he'd say, "where do you get all those
women?"

"you just gotta be around night and day," I told
him

and that was it, that was half of being a ladies'
man

the other half was letting it happen.

yrs., Anica

she used to write me little notes
on yellow paper with blue lines.
the yellow paper would be torn from
a ringed notepad,
carelessly.
and the paper would be folded many
times into a hard mass
and when I pulled it out of the
envelope it would say something
like: "Dear Hank: I am now
working in this factory and living
with my cat Desmond. . .
            yrs., Anica."
I don't know where she got my address
or what she wanted
I got these letters from small towns
in Louisiana and Texas.

"Dear Hank: I am tired of this
town and am moving soon. . .
            yrs., Anica."

"Dear Anica," I wrote her once,
"I am still drinking and playing
the horses. . ."

then I got a note from her saying that
she would be at the Greyhound bus stop,
Los Angeles, at 8 a.m. on a certain
morning and that she had an hour
stopover on her way to Berkeley but
she'd like to see me.

on that morning I got up
in the early a.m. and drove down
to the Greyhound station and sat on the bench
with the people and waited.

I didn't know what she looked like
but a young sexy one got off with
this guy talking into her ear and
I knew it was her and as I walked up
and took her suitcase the guy
vanished.

"You're Anica," I said, "are you
sure you've only got an hour?"

"Yes, Hank."

pure long blond hair
perfect skin
green-blue eyes
graceful of figure
was she.

I took her around the corner
for breakfast.
as we had juice and scrambled
eggs
our knees pressed together
under the table.

"You got a kind face,"
she told me.

"But it's old,"
I said.

"Yes, it is," she said.

I walked Anica back to the Greyhound station
and we waited for her boarding call.
when it came she stood up and
said, "Come over here a moment,"
and she took me around the corner
where there were few people
and I kissed her goodbye.
then I put her on the Greyhound. . .

a few weeks later I got a letter
from Berkeley
which I didn't answer.
some months went by and
I got a letter
from a small Texas town:

"Dear Hank: I got this job
I hate but it's only
3 hours a day and I have this
little place with a garden
in back and I work in the
garden. . .
              yrs., Anica."

there were 2 or 3 other letters
none of which I answered,
the last, I believe, from
some small town in
Louisiana.

she was the most beautiful
woman
I have ever met.

rock

here were all these males tuning their guitars
not a woman around
and they were content with that.
then they started arguing about who was best
and what was wrong with the so-called best.
and a couple of them had been famous
and they sat there on my rug
drinking my wine and beer and smoking my
cigarettes.

two of them stood up
to duke it out
and that's when I ran them all off
with their guitars and their guitar cases
out into the moonlight
still arguing.

I closed the door.
then I leaned against the couch and drained a beer
fast and I
gagged:
not a very good night:
it was full of
ashes.

night school

in the drunk driver's class
assigned there by division 63
we are given tiny yellow pencils
to take a test
to see if we have been listening
to the instructor.
questions like: the minimum sentence for a
2nd drunk driving conviction is:
    a) 48 days
    b) 6 months
    c) 90 days
there are 9 other questions.
after the instructor leaves the room
the students begin asking the questions:
"hey, how about question 5? that's a
tough one!"
"did he talk about that?"
"I think it's 48 days."
"are you sure?"
"no, but that's what I'm putting
down."
one woman circles all 3 answers
on all questions
even though we've been told to
select only one.

on our break I go down and
drink a can of beer
outside a liquor store.
I watch a black hooker
on her evening stroll.

a car pulls up.
she walks over and they
talk.
the door opens.
she gets in and
they drive off.

back in class
the students have gotten
to know each other.
they are a not-very-interesting
bunch of drunks and
x-drunks.
I visualize them sitting in a
bar
and I remember why
I started drinking
alone.

the class begins again.
it is discovered that I am
the only one to have gotten
100 percent on the test.

I slouch back in my chair
with my dark shades on.
I am the class
intellectual.

platonic

she wanted a platonic afternoon and I said, all right
but what can we do?

and she said, I like to talk.

so I took her to the racetrack and we
talked.
she had on an Indian headband
and she talked about literature
and I talked about horses.

she was going to teach poetry back
east.

after the races she mentioned that she
liked this Spanish place, the food was
really good, and since I had won $65 at
the track I thought we might as well.

the décor was Spanish
the food was Mexican and
the man at the piano sang American songs
in English,
loudly.

we ordered drinks and dinner
and she talked at high pitch
with volume
so that I could hear her over
the singer and the piano.

she screamed: I am really looking

forward to teaching! I've wanted to
do something like that ever since the
children grew up!

I screamed: ah ha!

I was getting a headache.

she screamed: do you think poetry
can be taught?

I screamed: no!

she screamed: I think I can do it!

I screamed: care for another drink?

*

back at my place I brought out some vodka
and 7.

someday, she screamed, I am going to
isolate myself! I'm going to be *alone*
and really get some writing done!

she was still screaming even though
the man at the piano was far away.

as she made various proclamations
she whirled about, a semi-dance
with much arm-waving. at times she
laughed frantically and slapped
my legs and pinched them.

the gods will not deny me!
she screamed.

I'll walk you to your car, I
told her, this neighborhood is
full of rapists.

oh, thank you, she said.

after she got in the car
and started the engine
she leaned out the window
kissed me on the cheek.
and drove off.

well, like they said:
sex wasn't everything.
there was the soul too.
I walked back into my place
and started looking for
mine.

hello, Barbara

25 years ago
in Las Vegas
I got married
the only time.

we were only
there an hour.
I drove all the
way up and all
the way back
to L.A.

I still
didn't feel
married and
I continued
to feel that way for 2 and
½ years until
she divorced
me.

then I found
a woman
who had ants
for pets and
fed them
sugar.
I got her
pregnant.

after that

there were
many other
women.

but the
other day
this man
who has been
looking into
my past
said, "I've
got the
phone number
of your
x-wife."

I put it
in my
dresser
drawer.

then I got
drunk one
night
pulled the
number out
and
phoned her.

"hey, baby,
it's *me*!"

"I know it's
you," she said
in that same

chilly
voice.

"how ya
doin'?"

"all right,"
she answered.

"you still
livin' on that
chicken ranch?"

"yes," she
said.

"well, I'm
drunk
I just thought
I'd give you
a little
call."

"so you're
drunk again,"
she said in
that same
chilly voice.

"yes. well,
all right,
I'm saying
goodbye now. . ."

"goodbye," she
said and hung

79

up.

I walked over
and poured a
new drink.
after 25 years
she still
hated me

I didn't think
I was that
bad.

of course,
guys like me
seldom
do.

genius

he
usually wore a vest and
a coat no matter
how hot it was
and his clothes were
always dirty
except for a colorful
clean scarf

no matter how many times
I moved
he always managed
to find me
for my couch
and the booze

and he'd drink
and he'd tell me
of his genius
recite
a few new poems
from memory

pass out
and sometimes
during the night
puke on the rug

afterwards snoring
keeping me awake
most of the
night

he'd jump up
at 6 a.m.
and take walks
around the
block

always coming back
with wild stories
about hookers
or
dead bodies in
the gutter

in a loud voice
while smoking cigarettes
that dangled,
he'd begin again
about his genius

"if I were a
fag or a black
I would make
it!"

pacing
the floor

"if I were a
black fag Jew
I'd make it!"

well
he was a Jew
so he'd
make it

one-third of
the way

at other poet's
poetry readings
he'd leap up on
stage
and read his
own things

he hustled so
hard
that people
hid
from him

"this panhandling
has got to be
wearing," I told
him, "why don't you
get a job and
write
on the side?"

"NO!" he screamed,
"I GOTTA BE RECOGNIZED!"

he was good
he was a very good
writer
but like the rest of
us
he wasn't as good
as he thought
he was

I'm sorry
but I was always
glad
when he left.

overt population

I'll say one thing: her older sister wrote
more novels than anybody I ever knew but
the novels kept coming back. I read some
of them, or rather—parts of them. maybe
they were good, I didn't know, I wasn't a
critic: I didn't like Tolstoy or Thomas
Mann or Henry James.
anyhow, her novels kept coming back and
her men kept leaving, and she just ate more,
had more babies; she didn't bathe and seldom
combed her hair and she let the diapers lay
about stinking. and she talked continually
and laughed continually—a highly nervous
laugh—she talked about men and sex
continually and I never criticized her because I sensed she had enough trouble and
I was living with her younger sister, besides.

but one afternoon when we were visiting, the
older sister said to me: "all right, I know
you've had some novels published but I have
these babies, these children, that's an art,
that's *my* art!"

"many people have babies," I said, "that's
really not exceptional, it's rather standard.
but to write a good novel is a rare and an
exceptional thing."

she leaped up and waved her arms: "oh yeah.
oh yeah? what about *your* daughter? where
is *your* daughter now?"

"Santa Monica, California."

"'SANTA MONICA? WHAT THE HELL KIND OF FATHER
ARE YOU?"

I no longer see either sister, although
about 2 months ago the younger one phoned
long distance and among other things she
told me that her sister had just mailed
her latest novel off to New York and that
her sister thought it was very good, that
it was the one, that it was the one that
would do it.

I didn't tell her younger sister that
all of us novelists think that and that
is why there are so many of us.

out of the mainstream

after Mickey's wife goes to work
he walks to the back of the court and starts smoking dope
with Harry the house painter.
Harry the house painter has a cowed dog named
"Pluto"
who whines away the day
at the end of a long rope.

I can't blame anybody: people get tired of the
mainstream

I sit inside my place
reading the daily newspaper over and over
again.
then I turn on the tv to the
morning soap operas
and I am glad that I don't live
with any of those women
they are always getting pregnant and are
always unhappy
with their doctors and lawyers.

I snap the set off
consider masturbating
reject that and
take a bath instead.

the phone rings, it's my
girlfriend: "what are you
doing?"

"nothing."

"what do you mean, 'nothing'?"

"I'm in bed."

"in bed? it's almost noon."

"I know."

"why don't you take a walk?"

"all right. . ."

*

I get up, get dressed and go outside.
I walk south down Western
I walk all the way to Santa Monica Boulevard
go into Sears-Roebuck.

there's a blue jean sale on.
I purchase a pair for under $10.
I take the escalator down
and in the candy section
I buy a large bag of popcorn.

then I stroll through the hardware section
looking at tools that I have no interest in,
then to the electrical section
where I stand looking at a series of
sunlamps,
jamming the popcorn into my mouth
and feeling like a total
asshole.

time is made to be wasted

I had just bought some boxer shorts
and a pair of blue jeans
and I had just purchased a box of popcorn
and was walking by the shoe dept.
when I heard the salesgirl say to the
man seated,
"I'm here to help fit you
into some shoes. you needn't get
personal."
the man was old with a bent back
and grey hair.
"all right, all right," he said.

when I got to the parking lot
2 cars were crashed together
and the young man in a new car was
saying to the lady in the old car,
"madam, why did you do that? look
at my poor car."
the woman was built like a
linebacker for the Dallas Cowboys
and she screamed:
"OH SHUT UP! SHUT UP, YOU DUMB SON
OF A BITCH!"

I ate the popcorn in the car
and drove home. the phone was
ringing.
"hello," I answered.

"where've you been?" she asked.
"I've been ringing and ringing."

89

"I went shopping."

"shopping?"

"yes. . ."

"you haven't been to see
Cupcakes, have you?"

"no, besides she's moved to
Glendale."

"Glendale? how do you know?"

"now, come on. . ."

"I want to *know*. . ."

"I got some boxer shorts and
some blue jeans."

the night was a little better
than the day. the police helicopter
circled overhead, they had
an apartment house on
Serrano Avenue
staked out.
the police crouched behind bushes
with rifles and shotguns and pistols
and they brought out one man in a
white shirt
the blood ran down the front of him
a red mess
and he was handcuffed in
back. there were one or two others still

90

inside and the police threatened them
over a loudspeaker. . . .

strangely, I lost interest
and as I walked back toward
my place
I got a toothache
and I didn't have many teeth
left
and suddenly a grey crippled cat
ran across the sidewalk in front of
me
its back arched
tail high
I saw its bunghole in the moonlight
and then it vanished under a

bush.

'e've got to communicate

"he was a very sensitive man," she told me, "and after
he split with Andrea he kept her panties under his
pillow and each night he kissed them and cried.
look at you! look at that expression on your face!
you don't like what I just said and do you want to
know why?
it's because you're *afraid*; it takes a man to admit
his feelings.
I see you watching women getting in and out of their
cars, hoping their skirts will climb up so you can
see their legs.
you're like a schoolboy, a peep-freak!
and *worse* than that, you just like to *think* about
sex, you really don't want to *do* it, it's only
work to you, you'd rather stare and imagine.
you don't even like to suck my breasts!
and you don't like to see a woman doing things in the
bathroom!
is there something *wrong* with bodily functions?
don't *you* have bodily functions?
Jesus, Christ, my sisters warned me about you!
they told me what you were like!
I didn't believe them, hell, you *looked* like a
man!
all your books, thousands of poems, and what do you
know?
you're afraid to look at a woman's pussy!
all you can do is *drink*!
do you think it takes any guts to drink?
here I've given you 5 years of my life and what do you
do?: you won't even *discuss* things with me!
you're charming enough when we have a party, that is,

92

if you're in the mood
you can really talk your shit
but look at you now, not a sound out of you, you just
sit in that chair over there and pour drink after
drink!
well, I've had it, I'm going to get myself somebody
real, somebody who can discuss things with me,
somebody who can say, 'well, look Paula, I realize
that we are having some problems and maybe
if we talk about them we can understand each other better
and make things work.'
not *you*! *look* at you! why don't you *say* something?
sure: DRINK IT DOWN! that's all you know how to do!
tell me, what's wrong with a woman's pussy?
my mother left my father because he was like you,
all he did was drink and play the horses!
well, he almost went crazy after she left him.
he pleaded and pleaded and pleaded for her to come
back, he even pretended he was dying of cancer just
to get her to come see him.
that didn't fool her—she went and got herself a decent
man, she's with him now, you've met him: Lance. but no,
you don't *like* Lance, do you?
he wears a necktie and he's into real estate. . .
well, he doesn't like you either. but mother loves him.
and what do *you* know about love?
it's a dirty word to you! *love.* you don't even 'like'!
you don't like your country, you don't like movies, you
don't like to dance, you don't like to drive on freeways,
you don't like children, you don't *look* at people,
all you do is sit in a chair and drink and figure systems
to beat the horses and if there's anything duller and
dumber than horses, you let me know, you just tell
me!

all you know how to do is to wake up sick each morning,
you can't get out of bed until noon; you drink whiskey,
you drink scotch, you drink beer, you drink wine, you
drink vodka, you drink gin, and what does it mean?
your health gets worse and worse, your left thumb is
dead, your liver is shot, you have high blood pressure,
hemorrhoids, ulcers and Christ knows what else,
and when I try to talk to you, you can't take it
and you run to your place and take the phone off
the hook and put on your symphony records and drink
yourself to sleep, and then you wake up sick at noon
and phone and say that you're dying and that you're
sorry and that you want to see me, and then I come over
and you're so *contrite* you're not even human—
oh, you can be *charming* when you're sick and in trouble,
you can be humorous, you can make me laugh, you win me back
again and again. . .
but look at you *now*! all you want is one more drink and then
one *more* drink and you won't talk to me, you just keep
lighting cigarettes and looking around the room. . .
don't you *want* to work at making our relationship better?
tell me, why are you afraid of a woman's pussy?"

the fast life

she threw all my clothes out the front door—
shoes, shirts, dirty underwear, razor, photos,
stockings, so forth
and she screamed,
"GET OUT! GET OUT! GET OUT!"

it was her house
and it was one-thirty in the afternoon
and it was about the night before
(a party)
and I was very sick.

"don't you remember what you did last
night?"

"no. . . ."

that had been the theme
since 10 a.m.
me
sitting
listening.

"you always want to make me feel bad!
well, I'll tell you, you know how to do
it!
you really know how to make a woman feel
bad!"

"uuuh?"

"come on, talk to me! why don't you *talk*

to me?
you sure know how to talk at night with all
those people around, I NEVER heard a talker
like you in all my life!"

my car was down there and I gathered up
my belongings bit by bit and threw them into
the car.
I tossed a pair of unmatched dirty stockings
into the rear seat
as the squad car drove up.

"hey, buddy, what're you doing?"

"moving."

"you're not stealing that stuff are you?"

"nobody would steal this stuff."

just then my radio came flying through the air.
it hit the sidewalk and smashed apart.

"THERE'S YOUR FUCKING RADIO!" she screamed.

I left it there and drove off.
the law didn't follow me. . .

I found a nice motel
just above Hollywood and Western,
swimming pool and color tv,
liquor store just downstairs
got three six-packs
sat in the bed
cracking cans and not feeling

bad at all
tv on:
people in various sorts of trouble,
man and woman stuff.
the total indifference of a motel room
was a gentle vacuum.
I'd stay a week
sit in various nudey bars
then find an apartment
unlisted phone
lay quiet
look for a job. . .
I finished one six-pack
got sleepy,
slept. . . .

to be awakened by this knocking
and when I opened the door
it was her
I walked back to the bed
and climbed in as she closed the
door.

"I've decided that I can't live
without you," she said.

so I got dressed and we went back
to her house
my car following her car
me sucking at a beer can,
and at each signal
her giving little signs out the window
making faces in her rear view mirror.
I wondered how she had found me
and worse,

why she didn't want to let me go
because I knew that soon
I would be back in another motel room,
only next time
I'd check the rear view mirror
on the way.

I am a reasonable man

I had flown a thousand miles to see her
at her request
"just for old time's sake."

we'd had the night together
and now it was breakfast
in this Arizona cafe,
nice quiet place
the sun coming in
on the red and white checkered
tablecloth.

she said,
"I can't eat. . ."

the tears were running down
her face

"I'll finish your breakfast,"
I told her,
"no use wasting it. . ."

she straightened her back
inhaled and
screamed.

the waitress and the
fry cook
came running out.

"is everything all right?"
the waitress asked.

"oh yes,"
I answered.

they both went
in back
and watched us
through the serving
window.

across from me
her tears were still
coming

"have a bite of bacon,"
I told her,
"you'll feel better."

"shut up,"
she said,
"just shut up!"

"look," I told her
"I'll leave today."

"let's try
one more night,"
she said,
"we can talk. . ."

I finished her
breakfast, paid and
we left.

*

that night we
drank and talked and
then slept.

about 3 a.m.
I awakened
howling in pain

she had grabbed
my balls
and yanked.

"you crazy bitch,"
I said,
"what's the matter
with you?"

"you didn't fuck me,
you didn't fuck me,"
she said.

I got up and began
dressing.

"what are you
doing?" she asked.

"doing? doing?" I
pulled my pants up,
"I'm going to catch
a cab
to the airport!"

I sat down
and began putting

my shoes on.

then she
was out of bed and
in between my knees
unzipping me.

"I want you to
stay,"
she said,
bending her head down
toward my center.

"I want you to
stay,"
she said

"all right,"
I said,
as the summer moon
came
through the curtains,
"just for old time's
sake."

free coffee

it was on the telephone and he said, look, I'm with
Lisa now, I can't do that—
and she said, I know, I understand, I just want you
to come and have coffee with me, I'm one
block away on Western, I just got in from Utah, I just
thought we'd have coffee for old time's sake—
he said, all right
then he said to Lisa, be back in five minutes—

he got into the Volks and drove and there she was
sitting in her car and he got in and she had two coffees
waiting there outside of Pioneer Chicken.

hi, she said. hi, he said.

you know, she said, you are the only man who can make
me laugh. you're really funny and I miss that.

yeah, he said.

how's it going? she asked.

fine, he said, real good.

you know Cal? she asked. well, he
turned out to be a god damned fag. it's bad enough
to be competing with other women, there I was competing
with men. . .

I think I've lived with a couple of lesbians, he said,
but I'm not sure.

I really miss you, she said.

look, he said, I've got to be getting back.

I understand, she said, then leaned over and kissed
him.

see you, he said, and got out of her car and walked to
the Volks and as he drove off she was still sitting
in her car and he waved and she waved back. . .

it was a perfect day in July and he walked back in
to Lisa sitting straight upright in a chair
as if she had been frozen for rebirth at a better time.

laugh

best was the time we were driving along after not seeing
each other for some time.
you had asked to see me, you wanted to be driven somewhere.
your car had been stolen. no, it wasn't that: it was the
carburetor or you needed a tune-up. anyhow, we drove along
and stopped at a signal on Los Feliz, and your hair was
all combed out and you said, "I'm with Paul now."
I laughed. I hadn't laughed that well for months, in years.
then I checked myself: was it a purposeful laugh to annoy
you? or was it just relief?
so I checked inside and found it hadn't been defensive:
it just felt good to clean everything up. so
we ran your errand and went someplace to eat, and I suggested
that the pre-meal drink be to Paul who had no idea of what
was coming to him, and you said that he had no idea of
what you were getting away from, so we
drank to that. then we had another drink with no toast.
I always liked your hair combed out like that and you always
knew just where to put the ribbon.

meeting is more exciting than parting but parting is
important if you want to stay alive in a certain way.
never again will I see all of your beauty sleeping, wide-
legged, immune to me: we've all been cheated.

old Butch, they fixed him
the girls don't look like much
anymore.

when Big Sam moved out
of the back
I inherited big Butch,
70 as cats go,
old,
fixed,
but still as big and
mean a cat as anybody
ever remembered
seeing.

he's damn near gnawed
off my hand
the hand that feeds him
a couple of
times
but I've forgiven him,
he's fixed
and there's something in
him
that doesn't like
it.

at night
I hear him mauling and
running other cats through
the brush.

Butch, he's still a magnificent
old cat,
fighting
even without it.

what a bastard he must have been
with it
when he was 19 or 20
walking slowly down
his path
and I look at him
now
still feel the courage
and the strength
in spite of man's smallness
in spite of man's scientific
skill
old Butch
retains
endures

peering at me with those
evil yellow eyes
out of that huge
undefeated
head.

maybe we'll see . . .

sometime soon
they are going to shoot a telescope
from the shuttle platform out there
and the boys and girls are going to see
ten percent more outer space,
things
they have never seen before.

I am for this.

our inventiveness
our poking around
is pleasurable.

it makes a peanut butter and
jelly sandwich taste
better.

it is having such things to do
which keeps us
from doing things
to ourselves.

pretty boy

we drank together
I was 59 and he was 29
and he could catch girls
like a spider caught flies
only faster than that:
he didn't have to wait.

he was a pretty boy,
well, he wasn't pretty to
me,
just to the girls—
slim body, tight-fitting
clothes,
blue eyes, blond locks,
perfectly-shaped
ears, nose, chin and so
forth.
also, one of his x-wives
told me he had a
big cock.
besides that, he had a
private income.

he held a mixed drink
while I sucked on
beer after beer.

"when my old lady
goes out to fuck somebody,"
he said,
"I just put on my pajamas,
pull up the covers and

go to sleep."

"I can't do that,"
I said.

"it's just a *hole*,"
he said,
"you worry too much
about it."

he got up and
changed the record
on his stereo.
he moved like a gazelle.
there were no wrinkles
in his pants,
no spots or stains.
he was like something off a drawing board.

my pants—
the pockets ripped open
the zipper didn't go
to the top
the belt too long and curled,
cigarette holes—
my pants were either
too long and
I stepped on them
with my heels
or they were too short
and showed stockings
which didn't cling.

he turned the stereo up
loud,

came back and
sat down.

"with women," I told him,
"I get attached,
I get sentimental."

he grinned at me
showing even white teeth.

"you know," I said,
"her pillow next to my
pillow; my car pushing
her stalled car down the
street; and when it rains,
you know, we listen to the
same rain from the same
bed. I could make
a long list. . ."

his grin increased.
he knew my women;
he had managed to get to bed
with most of them.

"I don't like your women,"
he told me.

he got up
moved into his kitchen
and mixed himself a
fresh drink.
he had seltzer bottles,
and machinery which
hummed and clicked and

whirled.

he stood a moment
under the kitchen light
his hair looking more
golden than ever.
then he walked out
with a glass tube
sticking out of his
drink.
the tube had little
colored veins
running through it.
he sat down and
stirred his drink
with the glass tube.

"o.k.," he said,
sipping at his drink,
"first, you don't dress
right, you got to wear
tight pants so your
cock shows."

"wait a minute,"
I said, "I'm almost
60 years old. . ."

"just listen to me,"
he said, "they got to
see the cock, they like
to see it, and if you
don't have a big cock
you wear a dildo,
lots of guys do it.

and it doesn't matter
because once you
get into them it's
too late for them.
and you've got to
learn to dance
because women relate
dancing to fucking.
they think if you can
dance good
you can screw good."

"is there," I asked,
"some truth in that?"

"of course not," he
told me, "but truth has
nothing to do with
this thing."

"is there any more beer?"
I asked.

"down by your foot," he said,
"you brought three six-
packs, remember?"

I said, "this beer is
kind of warm."

"with a woman," he continued,
"you must always make yourself
seem to be
unavailable.
you must act disinterested;

113

once she's solved you she's
done with you;
she needs a problem to
work on."

"why don't you turn that
god damned stereo down
a bit?" I asked.

"just remember," he said,
"there are 6,000 boats
at Marina del Rey
with at least
two beautiful whores
on each one of them
and you'll never have
any of them."

"I've got to go,"
I told him.

"o.k.," he said,
"be cool, man. . . ."

I walked down through
the court and
before I could get
to my door I had to
stop and vomit in the bushes.

I finished
opened my door
and went inside
and there was the bed
and there were the walls

hello
and the problem was
that it had happened before.
I went to the refrigerator
and found
a cold beer,
cracked it.

if you got up
in the morning
and if you had a
car on the street
and if that car
hadn't been stolen
and if you
got into it
and it started
then that was
miracle enough.

I drank the
cold beer.

the new woman

you are sitting with the new
woman
you've worked out the sex thing
all right
it's the 3rd or 4th night
now you're becoming friends
talking about this and that

she has a nice place
plenty to eat. . .
also books, magazines, drapes,
dried figs, oranges and the
like.
she smokes and laughs
much.

so you've done with one
woman
and here's another
one.
maybe she likes somebody
who lays around and doesn't
do much.

all right.
more to drink
more to say.

she gets into her x-
man.

oh, that one beat you?

this one took drugs?

that one couldn't get it
up anymore?

I understand. . .

the last was who? Billy
Thong? why did you tell
me?

you mean you really lived
with *Billy Thong*?

listen, I went to jail one
night with that filthy swine.

a matter of busted door glass
at my x-girl friend's place.
I busted out eight panes,
he got one.

they put us in the same
tank.

he was so disgusting the others
in the same tank
wanted to kill him.
they should have.

I saved his ass by
explaining him
away.

oh fuck Billy Thong,

she says, and let's get on
with us.

yeah, I say.

I like you, she says,
you admire Carson McCullers
and James Thurber and you're the
first man I've found who has admired
both of them.

I'll be right back,
I tell her,
and I go into one of her
bathrooms and piss.

it's strange about her
bathrooms
one bathroom has extra rolls
of toilet paper
and the other has none.
I found out about the bathrooms
the first morning
I was in the wrong one
staring at the little naked grey
cardboard roll.

I finish pissing and walk out to
see her again.

she crosses her legs and lights a
cigarette: I'm sorry about Billy
Thong, let's forget him.

all right, I say,

thinking
I will eat all the food in this
place, I will smoke the cigarettes
and drink the booze and then I'll
sleep with her but I won't fuck her
and when she's still asleep in the
morning I will sneak out of bed and
get down there to my car parked in
back
maybe taking a few cans of beer
from the fridge

and then I'll go south on
Vermont
take a right
go west to my place
get in there
take the phone off the
hook,
undress,
get into my own bed
pull the covers
up to my throat
and start
all over again
feeling cheated because
Billy Thong had killed it
before I could.

we both knew him

I knew him before I knew you, she said
in bed afterwards, he was always talking
about you, he loved your writing and he
introduced me to your books and now
we're lovers. . .
you know, he slashed his wrists several
times and just recently had himself
committed, did you know him?

yes, I said, we were in the drunk tank
together. the other prisoners wanted to
kill him but I gave a speech and talked
them out of it.

I used to think he was a genius, she said,
every morning when he awakened he would
leap up in bed and scream out,
"how do you like your blue-eyed boy,
Mister Death?"
later I found out who wrote
that. . .

cummings.

yes, she said, that's when we
split, when I found that
out.

how long were you with
him?

2 years. he talked about you
all the time. Chinaski, Chinaski,
Chinaski . . . and now *we're* together
and we're lovers. . .

yes, I said, where's the bathroom?

straight ahead through that door
in front of us there. . .

I got up, went in, pulled down my
pants, sat down, thinking, fucking
often has nothing to do with being
"lovers" and fucking seldom has much
to do with literature and literature
has nothing to do with fucking except
to write about it when more important
things give way, and most literature
is pretty fucking bad.

when I finished I washed up and
climbed back into bed with her
whereupon she kept rubbing one of
her thighs against mine.
she wanted it again.
and
she wanted to teach me how to
dance, I didn't dance well, I
didn't dance upon the balls of
my feet.
and she liked Greece, she liked to
talk about Greece.

come on, she said, this balcony is
just like Greece, follow me.

and we stood there on the balcony
naked with the cars rolling up and
down the boulevard I could feel the
air and the sun about my nodules.
we stood there. she had false teeth
and kept lighting cigarettes and
talking and I had no idea what to
do with her.

then she reached down and grabbed
my piece.
I took her wrist and from underneath
pressed my thumb against her veins
until the hand opened.

I told her it was too god damned
early in the morning
for that.

I went in and got dressed and I
knew I would see her one more
time and that
would be it.

discard or be discarded.
it was endless.

she gave me a copy of the
New Yorker and a six-pack
of beer and, Mister Death,
I left.

killer

it was one of those days,
he told me, I had a fight
with my wife, a bad one,
I just had to get out of
there so I jumped in the
car and backed out the
driveway and ran over the
god damned cat, I heard it
scream and when I got out
of the car it was
laying there
its guts punched–out
coming out of its mouth
but it was still alive
looking at me
and then my wife ran out
and yelled at me,
"YOU'VE MURDERED THE
CAT! YOU'VE MURDERED THE
CAT!"
"NO," I yelled back, "IT'S
STILL ALIVE!"
the cat was totally crushed, flat
but still breathing.
I ran and got the
nearest thing I could
find, a shovel, and I
started beating it
over the head
and my wife
grabbed at me

123

and ripped my shirt
and ripped me.
"NO! NO! NO!" she
screamed.
"GET AWAY, YOU WHORE!"
I yelled and shoved her
to the asphalt.
I beat at the cat's head
with the shovel as
the little boy
next door
watched me.
then the cat was
finally dead.
the little boy ran off
toward his house
yelling, "MAMA! MAMA!
MR. SUMMERS JUST KILLED
HIS CAT!"

my wife got up
from the asphalt
and said,
"I never want to
see you again."
I got in the car
and drove off.

what are you
going to do?
I asked him.

I guess I'll just
get a motel room
and get good and

drunk, he said.

it's strange seeing
you, I told him.
I thought maybe you
were dead, I haven't
seen you for so long.

I might as well be
dead, he said. by
the way, how's it
going with
you and Lyn?

it's going pretty
good, I said.

oh, he said.

he looked down
into his beer
and then finished it off.

o.k., he said,
I'm going.

take it easy,
I said.

then he was out the
door.

I'd given him the
last unwanted cut
by telling him

that it was
going pretty
good between
me and Lyn.

what the hell
did he think
I was doing
sitting in a dull
neighborhood bar
at 9:15 p.m.
drinking Jack Daniels
with beer
chasers?

I can't stop

people keep telling me
you know,
you ought to stop writing
racetrack poems,
you have no *idea*
how boring they are.

well, I was at the track
the other day
and I had to go in
and take a piss.
I unzipped and stood there
grabbing and groping
and tugging;
I tugged and I groped and
I grabbed
and the guy next to me
said:
"my god, you must really
have a lot of it. . ."
and I told him,
"nothing like that, sir,
I've got my shorts on
backwards."

I got it out
from underneath
and pissed half of it
down my leg.
then I went out
and caught a
six to one shot

who won
by four lengths.

this is just another
boring poem.

fasten your seat belts

at one time
I knew two airline stewardesses
and I heard a few
jet plane stories
and the one I remember
is when a famous singer
(he was a big sex symbol)
took one of the two stewardesses
into the crapper
and had intercourse with her,
and all the passengers knew
about it
and then he came out
sat down and started drinking.
he got drunk and told
everybody around that
the stewardess was a
"pig."
he kept drinking and
he kept saying it
over and over again,
that she was a
"pig."

anyhow, the flight ended
and he got off
and later the stewardess
discovered she had
v.d.

that's all there is

to that
except that one of the
stewardesses that I
knew
who lived in Long Beach
moved and vanished
and the other one is
now in a
madhouse in Germany

and I never slept
with either of them
and the famous singer
is now
no longer famous.

culture

she was a class bitch although all her
teeth were gone.
once married to one of the leading medical diagnosticians
in the world
she still had money and her education
quite classic and her background
likewise
she sat at her place
in front of her full bookcase background
hair down into crumbling face
into which was poured endless tumblers of
scotch and water
she liked to correct my pronunciation.

"now James Thurber," she said, "JAMES THURBER
and Ross, I think his name was, he was the editor
of the *New Yorker,* they used to sit around for
hours arguing about the use of the comma."

"yes," I said, "while other people were starving
to death."

"now CHIN-ASS-SKI," she said, "since when do *you* give a
    damn
about other people starving to death?"

out on her balcony she talked about Greece and I used
to like to imagine we were in Greece
because I was hiding at her place
hiding out there because I had
an insane girlfriend who was trying to kill me.

"do you like Ibsen?" she asked.

"he knew his women," I answered, "but I prefer Knut
Hamsun."

"oh, do you like Knut Hamsun? do you know that there
is a Knut Hamsun Society?"

"like Mahler, eh?"

"oh, do you like Mahler too?"

"yes," I said, flicking my ashes out over the balcony
of my imaginary Greek island.

we drank and drank and each morning I'd awaken
not sure where I was.
then I'd look over at the north wall and there would
be:
the giant two-foot white styrofoam "S" she had glued
there.

I found out my mad girlfriend had returned to Arizona
so I went back to my place and sat around drinking beer
and looking out the window while
sitting in my shorts
getting fatter and lazier
but generally feeling useful
when
one night
the phone rang
and really into her scotch and water was
"S"
who said,
"listen, you think you've been fucking me? well, you ain't

fucked me yet, let me tell you, you think you're such a
hot dog. . . I don't want to hurt your feelings but I gotta
tell you something: you ain't even PENETRATED me yet!"
I hung up.

I drank a beer. I drank another beer.
then I put on shoes, pants, shirt, drove my car off the
front lawn of my court and got over there.

she was home.
I joined her with the scotch.
she put on Shostakovitch's 4th which she knew I preferred
to the 5th.

"James Thurber," she said, "is a greater writer than you'll
ever be."

"I know that," I said.

I don't know when we went to bed
but with Rod Stewart on the record player
I made sure that time
I gave her a stinky horse fuck
sweat running down my back from the top of my head
and from under the armpits
the bed rattled like a crazy tambourine
her head bounced like a metronome out of kilt.

in the morning I got up
puked
walked into the other room and she was sitting in a
chair at 9:30 a.m. re-reading Carson McCullers.

"there's some beer in the fridge," she said.

there was a long stairway down from her upper flat
and I went down that stairway, and each separate step of
the stair had its own bit of worn rug and I greeted each
piece personally on the way down, each one different,
each with its own character and yet each not
meaning too much of anything at all.

I found my car parked in back.
I got it out of the lot
backed out
looked out
looked up
because I knew
and there she was in my Grecian window
hanging out:
"bye, CHIN-ASS-SKI!"

hair down partly across her face
cigarette stuck into lips
glass of scotch and water in one hand.

there was nothing else to do:
I waved goodbye.

the descent of the species

Sweet Mama,
she liked ice cream, candy bars
and chocolate doughnuts;
breakfast at her place was
lemon meringue pie and hot chocolate.

she was 20 years younger and
the weight settled on *me*
easier.
after a while
when we made love
my belly got in the way.

"you're not as good as you
used to be," she said.

"get on top," I told her.

I had to throw away all my clothes
and get larger ones.

I got so fat that even
her getting on top
stopped working.

that finished us. . .

*

the next one I met
was 30 years younger.

she took pills, drank
and went to bed
with everybody.
she worried me sick
and I couldn't eat
at all.

I had to throw away all my clothes
and get smaller ones.

"you look awful," she said and
ran away with a younger man. . .

*

the next one was about my age
and we sat around
her place and drank and talked
about what a terrible place
the world was.

we also drank at cafes
and while we were there
we ate.
I was soon back to
my normal weight.

then Sweet Mama
saw me one day
all slimmed–down and
asked me to
come back to her
and I did,
only I didn't move
back in,

I stayed at my
place.

and then the one
who was 30 years younger
saw me and
told me I was looking good
and she started coming
by

and I decided
I'd keep them both—
one to worry me sick
and slim me down
and the other to pump me
full of sweets.

but I screwed that up.
I met a 30-year-old
divorcée
from Texas
who looked like
Katherine Hepburn
and I went down there
where she introduced me
to the works of
de Sade.

yes

no matter who I'm with
people always say,
are you still with her?

my average relationship lasts
two and one half years.
with wars
inflation
unemployment
alcoholism
gambling
and my own degenerate nervousness
I think I do well enough.

I like reading the Sunday papers in bed.
I like orange ribbons tied around the cat's neck.
I like sleeping up against a body that I know well.

I like black slips at the foot of my bed
at 2 in the afternoon.
I like seeing how the photos turned out.

I like to be helped through the holidays:
4th of July, Labor Day, Halloween, Thanksgiving,
Christmas, New Year's.
they know how to ride these rapids
and they are less afraid of love than I am.

they can make me laugh where professional comedians
fail.

there is walking out to buy a newspaper together.

there is much good in being alone
but there is a strange warmth in not being alone.

I like boiled red potatoes.

I like eyes and fingers better than mine that can
get knots out of shoelaces.

I like letting her drive the car on dark nights
when the road and the way have gotten to me,
the car radio on
we light cigarettes and talk about things
and now and then
become silent.

I like hairpins on tables,
on the floor.
I like knowing the same walls
the same people.

I dislike the insane and useless fights which always
occur
and I dislike myself at these times
giving nothing
understanding nothing.

I like boiled asparagus
I like radishes
green onions.
I like to put my car into a car wash.
I like it when I have ten win on a six to one
shot.
I like my radio which keeps playing
Brahms, Beethoven, Mahler.

I like it when there's a knock on the door and
she's there.

no matter who I'm with
people always say,
are you still with her?

they must think I bury them in
the Hollywood Hills.

laid up

Eddie in the back court, I knew his wife
and I hadn't seen him for some weeks and I asked
her, "where's Eddie, Jan? I haven't seen Eddie
for a couple of weeks."
Eddie and Jan had two children; they had all come
from South Carolina so the people could hear
Eddie play his guitar and sing
but Eddie hadn't had much luck in Hollywood.

"you still writing dirty stories, Hank?"
she asked me.

"oh yeah," I said, "but don't you think he ought
to see a doctor?"

"oh no," she said, "he gets the sleeping sickness
right off and on. it passes."

Eddie was back there with all the shades down,
thick grey shades and the sun couldn't get through
and some green brush had come up and covered part
of the window, and it was hot outside and his kids
were running up and down the walk screaming but he
didn't know it.

I walked down to my place, sat down and typed a
dirty story.
and that's that part of it.

the other part of it is that one day I moved out
of that court and soon after they moved out too,
and now and then I'll come to town and drive past

that court, stop the car and look in there
at where I used to live and at where Eddie and Jan
lived in back, and all I can think of is
Eddie laying back in there with the big grey
shade pulled down, just laying back there while
the traffic signals were changing at Hollywood and
Western, while the hustlers were hustling and the
cops patrolling and the boys catching steel in
barroom fights, and during the car crashes
and while the helicopters were flying overhead, Eddie with the
sleeping sickness.

within my own madness

I have always been fascinated by Chinese armies
of the past,
by Adolph Hitler, slim young ladies in long dresses,
a checkerboard without pieces, flags of any country,
policemen of other countries, marmalade in the jar,
people standing outside of movie houses, men with one arm,
horses about ready to shit, how badly great actors act,
canaries at night, frogs in the center of a road,
bedsprings, whirling turds in a toilet,
paperclips, dark green, beds full of dying, betrayal,
fear, dark green freeway signs, chickens, chicken dung,
black traffic policemen, the deaths of presidents' wives,
how badly great actresses act, the failure of the poets,
the really really rich, the really really poor,
the murderers
and the murdered, the rapists and the raped

what my mother dreamt

within my own madness I have not been so fascinated by
myself, Italians, Jews, Englishmen,
the Women's Liberation Movement,
Spain, horse shows, the Pope, spinach, the sea,
the mountains,
the sunset

lemon trees fascinate me, palm trees do not
kindness fascinates me, love does not

preciseness fascinates me and the end of long-
windedness.

dead again

Ben phoned and said, "there's a rumor going around that
you're dead. *Hustler* magazine has gotten 3 or 4 calls
about that."
"well," I said, "maybe the dead can't tell, maybe finally I'm
dead. . . ."

5 years ago somebody started it:
"Bukowski's dead."

now it's beginning again.
they want me dead very much.
I seem to be very much on the minds of the death-wishers.
it's irritating to some
that a man nearing sixty
continues to write.
it should give them hope instead of
rancor.

I'll die, my friends, I have no doubt of
that

but I think that the history of our streets
would be less ugly
if we could celebrate men's lives
as well.

hell yes, I'll go. . .

I am standing around the track after the first race
no, it's before the first race and the mob rolls
and roars as two men are fighting and others are screaming
and a fat cop runs in, gets a punch in the face, yells,
"HEY, YOU SON OF A BITCH!", blows his whistle as the
    mass
of arms and yelling evolve toward me, one man breaks loose,
runs toward me making strange noises, I get ready to swing
but he circles off and the cop grabs him, blows his whistle
again.

I don't understand any of it, go over and buy a coffee,
drink it.

nothing much happens until just before the 6th race I am
standing two back in line watching the man at the window
doing his transactions with the teller and he's taking too
long and I don't like the shape of his head or his pants or
his coat, I don't like the way he stands, I pick up rays
from him that I realize *I* only feel, nobody else
feels this and I am telling myself, man, your sanity is
weakening, it's probably you who are the slime of the
universe, get it together, look the other
way, no single man should judge another. . . but I can't help
it: when he turns his lips are wet, his eyes glisten with
stupidity. . . we can judge but as we feel, not as
we are taught and told to do. . .
he took too long while they were putting them in the gate,
he actually relaxed, dawdled over his dumb selections,
calling all the wrong numbers. . .
I don't like the shape of his head or his pants or his
coat, I don't like his ears, his eyebrows, his shoelaces.

he stands and we stare at each other and we are enemies
from centuries back and I feel this proclivity to eliminate
him, we are locked. . .
I jerk my head up and down, make strange sounds that I have
never heard before. . . furious with nothing. . .
"yeh yeh yeh. . ."

one sound from him and I will be at his throat but he walks off
and I have time to buy a ticket just as they jump out of the
gate and I walk to the ramp as the numbers go by. the
mile-and-one-sixteenth race and the screaming begin, it's
always been a war.

a little sun

the whores at the All–American Burger
sit in the patio
laughing at 2:30 in the afternoon.
they have finished eating
and 2 of them are drinking coffee.
the 3rd drinks a coke through a straw.
the rains have stopped.
the rains have been terrible for business
everywhere.
I am reading the *Herald-Examiner*
at a corner table. the sun is on my back,
feels good. 2 of the girls
(the ones drinking coffee) are in pants;
the other one (drinking coke through a straw)
and facing me
wears a short skirt.
she spreads her legs and the sun
runs under the table and I can see her
panties:
they are a light blue.
I turn a page of the newspaper
see nothing
turn back to the front page:
the weatherman says there's
another storm on the way.
I get up and walk past their table.
they are giggling like
high school girls.

out on the sidewalk
a thin brown swayback dog with
bent long legs shivering

picks up half a dry bun
and tries to chew it;
the bun hangs out one side of
his mouth
as he tries to shuffle it down
his throat.

it hasn't been a very good
winter.

another day

getting the low-down blues and going into a restaurant
to eat, you sit at a table, the waitress smiles at you
she's dumpy. her ass is too big. she seems kind
and understanding.
live with her 3 months—a man would never know such agony
again.
o.k., you'll tip 15%.
order a turkey sandwich and a beer.
the man at the table across from you has a head like an
elephant.
at a table further down are 3 men with tiny heads
like ostriches. they talk loudly of land development.
you think: why the hell did I ever come in here when
I've got the low-down blues?

the waitress comes with the sandwich and she asks you
if there will be anything else? and you tell her,
no no, this will be fine.
then somebody behind you laughs.
it's a cork laugh filled with sand and idiocy.

you begin eating the sandwich, it's something, it's
a minor, frustrating and sensible act like
composing a sap song that will make 14-year-old girls
weep

another beer.

Jesus, look at that guy, his hands come down almost to
his ankles and he's whistling.

well, time to get out.

pick up the bill.
tip.
go to the register.
pay.
pick up a toothpick
out the door.

your car is still there.
and there are the 3 men with heads like ostriches
getting into another car.
they each have a toothpick and are talking about women.

they drive away first. they're the best.
it's a first stage smog alert. all the birds are dead.
you start the engine.

a gallon of gas

"shit," said Wren, "we're out of gas!"
it was her car and she was always
running out of gas.
we were on the freeway and Wren coasted
to a stop at its edge.
we were in the car with her ten-year-
old daughter.

"mommy," said the little girl, "I
want to go home!"

"oh *shut* up, Adrienne!"

the lady's gas gauge didn't work.
she had a method of making marks
in the dust on the dashboard
to indicate how much gas she had
or didn't have.

I was beginning to understand better
and better why her husband had
recently divorced her.

"well," she laughed, "we'll just have
to walk.
I think I see a gas station over
there. . ."

we got out of the car and began walking
down the steep freeway slope through the
brush.
it was difficult but we were o.k. until

we were stopped by a tall chain link fence.

Wren stuck her pointed boot toes through the
wire and began climbing.
she got to the top, laughed, then jumped
to the other side.

"now you climb over," she said to me, "and
bring Adrienne with you."

"what?"

Wren looked at me through the fence.
"come on," she said, "hurry up!"

Adrienne hated me, she thought I had
stolen her mother from her father.

I reached down and picked her up.
she kicked and wiggled.
I felt my hand on her behind.

"you fat toad!" she spit at me.

she slapped me across the face.
I began to get an erection.
it was disgusting, I disliked
Adrienne.

"come on, Brad," her mother said
to me, "just don't *stand* there!"

Adrienne slapped me again and I bit
her on the side of the neck where
her mother couldn't see.

"you little bitch," I whispered.

then I took her under one arm and
started to climb.
the kid was kicking, she was
all wiggles, a little snake of a
girl.

I lost my grip and we fell back together.

Adrienne dropped on top of me and punched
me in the belly.
"you fat toad turd!"

I pushed her off and got up.
"listen, Wren," I told her mother, "I just
can't make it over with her, she's too big!"

"all right, you stay there and watch her.
I'll go get the gas!"

Wren started running toward the gas
station.

Adrienne looked at me.
"what's that thing sticking out in the front of your
pants, toad?"

"forget it. look, let's play hide and
seek!"

"no, I don't want to play hide and seek with
you! I HATE YOU!"

"let's fight then! if you hate me, hit

me! I won't hit back."

"promise?"

"I promise!"

I got down on my knees and she came on
in.
Adrienne had her little fists doubled and
she swung hard.

"toad! toad! toad!"

she was good, she really hurt me.

"now we'll wrestle," I said.

I grabbed her and we rolled over and over
in the grass.
Adrienne screamed, grabbed my hair and
spit in my face.

we rolled over and over.

then I pinned her down, I was on top
of her.

"you can't do anything now," I
said.

"you let me up!"

"maybe I won't!"

"let me up!"

"maybe. . ."

"here comes my mother!"

it was true, I could see Wren coming toward
us with a can of gas.
she was still far away but I got
up.

"I'm going to tell mommy that you *hurt*
me!"

"no, *no*, Adrienne! look, if you don't tell
I'll give you *five dollars!*"

"five whole dollars?"

"yes, but you must promise *never* to
tell!"

"I *promise*! give me the five dollars!"

"here! hide it!"

Adrienne took the five and hid it in her
panties.
her panties were a light blue.

then Wren came walking up to the
fence.

"Jesus, I'm *pooped*! here comes the
can!"

Wren was strong.

the gallon of gas came flying over the
fence.
then Wren followed

"I had to pay a five buck deposit on the
can but I guess I'll keep it."

"five bucks is a lot of money," I
said.

"yes, it is," said Adrienne.

I picked up the can and we all began walking
up the slope toward the car.

"I know you're pissed," said Wren, "about me
running out of gas again."

"it's all right," I said.

"you're not mad?"

"no. . ."

it was afternoon going into evening and
the freeway was a Stygian river of tin and
steel and unhappy people.

Adrienne ran ahead of us happily
singing some child's song and
skipping through the brush.

black and white roach

this headline in the Hollywood paper says,
WHORES AND PIMPS COME BACK LIKE ROACHES.
look, you think all these people have a nice
little place in the country? you think
they're going to bother to hustle their ass
if they have anything?
roaches? you know what reminds me of
roaches?: the black and whites cruising
everywhere, they aren't protecting anything,
they're just looking for a bust, looking to
get it off!
you can't go into a cafe anymore but
there's 3 or 4 of them sucking at coffee cups
trying to look pretty and macho.
those dumb motherfuckers were still sucking
mama's titties when they were four years
old.

look, Fedra, he said, how about another
drink?

sure. but I mean, she said, do you know where
I'm comin' from?

yeah. I also know where you're going, he
said, I'm busting your ass for trying to
hustle an undercover policeman.

they make you guys seem so human on tv,
she said, but you're nothing but a bunch
of mentally syphilitic pricks!

he pulled her out of the booth, pulled

both arms behind her back and put on
the bracelets, then he walked her out of
there like that, holding her arms very high,
wanting her to scream in pain, he bullied her
from the back, trying to coerce some sound,
he only made her stumble to the sidewalk as
somebody else's pimp picked up her purse
from the booth and walked back to the men's
room.

you can never tell who you're going to meet at any moment

she came up behind me and
tapped me on the shoulder
and there she was except the
face had hardened and
the breasts had almost
disappeared,
she wore an off-color
dress
and the eyes I had so often
seen alight with anger and joy
were listless
and she asked,
"how you doing, Turkey?"
and I told her, "well, I
still pass water. . .
how's it going with
you?"
"fine," she said, "just
fine."

we stood like that
and I thought, well, I must
look bad too.
of course, I've always looked
bad.

"you still writing those
poems?" she asked.

"and drinking. I can't stop
either habit, you alone?"

"married. he's in the men's
room."

"is he a jealous man?"

"nothing like you were."

"I always try to be best. . ."

we walked to the bar and she had her
usual vodka and tonic. I had one
too.

"Petey," she said, "is into
computers."

then Petey came out of the men's
room.
we shook hands and I bought him a
drink.

"Karen told me all about you,"
said Petey.

"and now you know about her. . ."

"like what?"

"she steals all the covers at
night. . ."

Petey drank his drink right down:
"who you got in the 6th?"

"Iron Mike. . ."

"he's a quitter. . ."

"yeah, I know. . ."

I finished my drink. "look
I'm going to leave you people in
peace. you ever get down around
Van Nuys, give me a call."

"we will, we will. . ."

I walked down the stairway to the first
floor ramp.
they were coming out for the post
parade.
Iron Mike looked good.

it was a Wednesday in July
and I thought,
I got away from her, I'm going to
bet $50 to win
just to celebrate. . .
Iron Mike looked good and
Delahoussaye was due.

the weather's been fair

now looking out toward town
nothing new
they've closed the horse trails
2 rapes and 3 murders in 4 weeks
snails frogs wild dogs everywhere
we need our own newspaper
it's nice to sit on the porch
it's best in the mornings
my dentist found nothing to pull Wednesday
he has hair on the backs of his hands
5 high school girls set fire to the janitor Monday
Martha says the skiff has a hole in the bottom
the wild dogs kill the domesticated dogs
they kill the hens and the cats
somebody stole my electric drill
Brad Evans probably
maybe I'll move to Monterey
all those high school girls think about is fucking
Jamie Boy, that's my cat's name
he eats his own fur like cotton candy
if we could get a main road through here we'd make progress
but time's made to be wasted
I've got 3 tv sets and nothing on any of them
snake-bite and crow blast, that's all we know
never had a god damned chance
daddy neither
I can roll a smoke with 2 fingers of my left hand
that's good enough for me.

on the hustle

I suppose
one of the worst times was
when
after a drunken reading and
an all night party
I promised to appear at
an eleven o'clock English
class
and there they sat
nicely dressed
terribly young
awfully comfortable.

I only wanted to sleep
and I kept the wastebasket
close
in case I
puked.

I think I was in the state of
Nebraska or Illinois or
Ohio.

no more of this,
I thought,
I'll go back to the factories
if they'll have me.

"why do you write?"
a young man asked.

"next question,"
I responded.

a sweet birdie with blue eyes
asked, "who are your 3
favorite contemporary
writers?"

I answered, "Henry Chinaski,
Henry Chinaski and Henry. . ."

somebody asked,
"what do you think about Norman
Mailer?"

I told them that I didn't think
about Norman Mailer and then I
asked, "doesn't anybody have a
beer?"

there was this silence, this
continuing silence and the class
and the prof looked at me and I
looked at them.

then the sweet birdie with
the blue eyes
asked,
"won't you read us
one of your poems?"

and then that's when I
got up and walked
out

I left them in there
with their prof
and I walked down

through the campus
looking at the
young girls
their hair
their legs
their eyes
their behinds. . .

they all look so good,
I thought, but
they're going to grow up
into nothing but
trouble. . .

suddenly I braced myself
against a tree and began
puking. . .

"look at that old
man," a sweet birdie with
brown eyes said to a sweet
birdie with pale green eyes,
"he's really
fucked-up. . ."

the truth, at
last.

attack and retreat

read to them
read to them and drink wine, let the young girls
dream of sucking your soul out of your cock
read to them
read to them and drink your wine, get paid in cash,
leave and let somebody else drive the car.
but before that
when you
read to them
read them the new ones so *you*
won't be bored
and when the applause comes
and the young girls look at you
with their hot bright eyes
remember when you were starving in small
rooms
remember the only time anybody wanted your
autograph was when you signed in
at the drunk tank
remember when other young girls thought you
were a roach.

read to them
read to them and drink your wine, and remember
all the poets who think that reading is
an important and a holy thing;
these are the poets who hate you,
these are the poets who read to 8 or 12 or
14 people.
these are the poets who write of
love and honesty and courage
or believe that they do.

leave the young girls to them, they need
the young girls for they have nothing
else.

take the cash and jam it
into your side pocket and get out and get away,
get back to your place, lock in.

you will be contacted: they'll want to issue a phonograph
record of the reading.

give the contract to your lawyer.

start in on novel #
4.

it's strange

it's strange when famous people die
whether they have fought the good fight or
the bad one.
it's strange when famous people die
whether we like them or not
they are like old buildings old streets
things and places that we are used to
which we accept simply because they're
there.
it's strange when famous people die
it's like the death of a father or
a pet cat or dog.
and it's strange when famous people are killed
or when they kill themselves.
the trouble with the famous is that they must
be replaced and they can never quite be
replaced, and that gives us this unique
sadness.
it's strange when famous people die
the sidewalks look different and our
children look different and our bedmates
and our curtains and our automobiles.
it's strange when famous people die:

we become troubled.

no chance in Pomona

on a half-mile track in a mile and one-sixteenth race
they go around twice from out of the chute.
another jock got thrown today just before the first
turn where he was stepped on once.
he was an unknown Mexican jock wearing orange silks
and he was flat upon his back, bleeding
and not moving.

nobody moved toward him, although he was near the
rail and the horses that were then on the backstretch
would have to come through again along the rail
where he was.

there were some moments while everybody waited for
somebody else
then a few, a very few,
3 or 4 men, jumped the fence and the outrider
rode up and sat there on his horse. the
field was coming around the curve and into the
stretch and the men, some of the men, grabbed the
jock by his legs and dragged him barely out of
the way as the horses ran by just inside of him.

by the time they got the jock into the ambulance
the winner-to-be came down the stretch the 2nd
time and crossed the wire at 16 to one as the
ambulance pulled away to the track emergency
room and the longest shot ran past around 3rd or
4th or 5th but it wouldn't show on the official
charts:

it was the horse without the jock:
the crowd had it figured right,
but not quite.

a poetry reading

look at them.
this place like a bar or nightclub.
sold out: poet and audience both
drunk

now and then a flashbulb
goes off.

the mike still doesn't work.
the poet sits.
a chance to drink some more.

a little girl comes up
sweet, sexy, psychotic
holds one of the poet's
books open to
autograph.
he writes. "I could rip you
apart. . ."
forgets to sign his name.
calls for another drink.

the mike works.

now the poet reads
feeling put-upon
forgetting he has agreed
to read for money.

after several poems
the poet stands up
announces:

"you god damn
shits,
you think this is
easy. . .
it's nothing but a
motherfucking
blood–letting. . ."

"GIVE US MORE BLOOD!"
screams a young boy
from the back.
it's the best poem
of the night.

the poet drinks
half a glass of
whiskey.
lights a cigar.
hacks.

sometimes they laugh
sometimes they applaud.
they confuse him
but most things do.

he drinks his way
to the finish.

there is applause
of relief.

then another sweet, sexy
psychotic girl comes
up to his table
says she

is from the local paper
would like to
ask some questions.

she
sits down.

he answers the first
question looking at her
hair and her eyes
imagining her
in bed with him.

"what do you think of F.
Scott Fitzgerald?"
she asks.

"I never," he answers,
"think of him. . ."
waving a hand in
emphasis
he spills a large beer
on her tight blue jeans,
saying,
"Jesus, Jesus, I'm
sorry. . ."
rubbing his hands
on her knees
along her wet thighs
as if to dry her.

she leaves and the
promoter arrives
with the money:
$432.

"shit," says the poet,
"you promised me $500."

"we had to pay two bouncers
$68 to keep the crowd
from
swarming all over you. . ."

"you mean I was that
good?" asks the poet.

"that bad," says the
promoter getting up
and leaving.

the poet pours another
drink.
grabs the mike:
"listen, I ain't finished
yet, I'm going to read you
another poem. . ."

somebody shuts the mike
off.
nobody protests.

the poet gets up
from his table
makes it to the men's
room
stands pissing.

a man next to him is
also pissing.

the poet says to the
man: "listen buddy, where
can I get a piece of ass?"

"I was going to ask you
the same thing,"
the man answers.

the reading is over.

true confession

now look Benny, he said
(blowing the cigar smoke into Benny's
face),
we don't want to circumvent the
truth, do we?

ah, no, said Benny

look, the only way I can defend you is
if you tell the truth.

sure. . .

then, tell me. . .

what?

you raped and killed this little girl,
right?

no, no, not me, it was somebody else. . .

you like little girls?

sure. . .
then you did it?

ah, no.

o.k., Benny, *I* did it. *you* defend
me.

I got no law training.

tell me, did you like it, Benny? what
did it feel like? he asked (blowing more
cigar smoke into Benny's face).

it was like eating an ice-cream cone. . . .

what flavor, Benny?

all the flavors. . . .

I'm not going to let them put you in the
chair, Benny, I'm going to get you life. . .

thank you, Mr. Markovitch. . . .

no thanks needed, Benny, I only do what I have to
do.

I guess we're both lawyers then, Mr.
Markovitch. . . .

pick six

the little old men:
what happened?

I see them at the
track.

this one
takes tiny steps
3 inches at a time
in old striped pants.

another
not so little
but old—
he looks like a
pregnancy
it all hangs down
over his belt
and he ignores it
although
it must be
⅓ of his body.

another is a
dwarf.
he is followed by
a prostitute who
keeps screaming at him,
"hey, Johnny, where the hell
you going?"
but Johnny keeps

walking in circles like
a wound-up toy
and he has a
large head and
it's more beautiful
than anything
I've seen in the
movies or
anywhere.

I look around and
there are these
aged and misshapen men
everywhere
walking about
talking
drinking coffee and beer
smoking. . .

there are
hundreds of them
but nobody notices
or if they do
they are gently
polite about it.

then
a man
walks up to me.
he is headless.
somebody
has sliced his head
entirely off and
I look down
into dark bubbles of

blood.
"hey, buddy,"
he asks, "where's
the nearest crapper?"

"over there," I tell
him, pointing.

how can he
talk?
how can he
see?
he walks off
toward the crapper.

they are
everywhere.
some have no
arms.
others
no eyes
no legs
no feet.
one has no
mouth
it's sucked in
dry like a
cat's bunghole.

they come to the
racetrack
every day
and I am
there too.
there aren't so

many women.
I don't know
where
the women go.

then
the dwarf comes
spinning by
his arms whirling
rapidly
he gives me a
good knock on
the knee
almost
flooring me.
"hey, Johnny," says
the prostitute, "where
the hell you going?"

people think that
all they have
at the racetracks
are horses. it's
not true. that's
why I come home
so tired
every night.

hair in the soup
blinkers don't work.
the usual insomnia.

pissed–off in traffic.
dead flowers.
dental appointment.

no auto insurance.
torn shorts.
roach in the radio.

sober neighbors.
lost space ship
boil on the neck.

dead cat on the boulevard.
de Sade grinning in the dark.
more trouble in the government.

supermarket line:
standing in torn shorts
with a boil on my neck.
getting an erection
looking at the girl cashier.
"how you doing?" she asks.
"I need my teeth drilled," I tell
her.

she doesn't answer.
she works the register
bags my groceries.

I pay her.
"have a nice day," she tells
me.

I walk out.
my erection goes down.

there's trouble in the government.
I didn't run over the cat.
all those people in the market will eat
tonight.
I will too but I won't sleep.

I go to my car.
the blinkers won't work
but it's only 2 p.m.
I'll use hand
signals.

does that girl cashier ever think of
sex?

hair in the soup.
dead flowers.
roach in the radio.
lost space ship.
no auto insurance.
I drive off as
de Sade grins in the
dark.

snap   snap

oh, the ladies can get snappish
sticking their hands into the sink
yanking at sheets
working their trowels through the earth
near the radish patch
sitting in the auto with you
as you drive along.

oh, the ladies can get snappish
discussing
God and the movies
music and works of art
or what to do about the cat's
infection.
the snappishness spreads to
every area of conversation
the voice-pitch remains at
high-trill.

what happened to the nights
before the fire
when they were all sweetness
of ankle and knee
pure of eye
long hair combed out?

of course, we knew that wasn't
real
but the snappishness is.
love is too
but it's stuck somewhere
between the crab apple tree

and the sewer.

the judge is asleep in his
chambers and
nobody's guilty.

suckerfish

Winthrop finds me where I am
sitting in the stands at the finish line.
"hi, Buck!" he says.
"Jesus!" I say.
Winthrop always startles me, when I see him
it's like a death ray being pointed
at me.
he is dressed in dirty polyester pants and
a red knit t-shirt with blue stripes.
he sits beside me smoking his pipe.
"how ya doin', Buck?" he asks.
I tell him that I am 30 or 40 dollars ahead.
he doesn't have a Racing Form, knows nothing about
horse racing and makes vague $2 bets on every race,
usually to place or to show.
he used to pester me in general admission;
to avoid him I'd gone from there to the
clubhouse and now he has found me again.
the horses come out for the post parade
and he says, "you know, you aren't getting into
any of the anthologies, I'm going to write something
about that."
Winthrop reviews books for the *L.A. Times*, writes
poetry and teaches retarded children.
he will be with me all afternoon.

Winthrop leaves for a moment and I have time to
check my figures and the tote board
Winthrop comes back with a ham sandwich,
potato salad and coffee.
he asks, "you heard from Zellerbach lately?"
Zellerbach is a friend of his who was once

editor of one of the leading sex mags.
"no," I answer.
Zellerbach has recently been canned but I hear
from the others there, they ring me
out of my hangover each morning:
"when ya gonna send us a story, Buck?"
people who call me "Buck" piss me;
I'm *Buke,* like in puke.

Winthrop asks, "how's your poetry coming,
Buck?"
I tell him that I rip off 6 or 8
every couple of nights.
he says, "that's good, that's good."
I tell him that I've got to go bet.

after laying my bet I decide to watch
the race on the television set.
as they are putting them into the gate
I notice that
Winthrop is standing beside me.

"Jesus Christ," I say, "I thought you liked to
watch them from the stands!"

Winthrop walks off in his duck-footed manner.
I watch the race: I lose by a nose
on a 6 to one shot.

when I get back to my seat Winthrop is
eating a coffee cake with coffee.

"you keep jamming that shit into your mouth,"
I tell him.
"that's all right," he says, "my weight's

all right."
"sure," I say.

"when you go to Italy," he says, "you ought to
demand that they pick you up in a
limousine. you're still going to Italy,
aren't you?"

"I think so. . ."

"you should have kept your old Volks. you
looked natural in that. somehow the BMW doesn't
suit you."

people like Winthrop have been worrying about
my soul for decades—I'm constantly informed
that I'm losing it or that I have lost it.
when a man loses his soul you don't tell him about
it, you stay away from him.

Winthrop says, "I was going to come over to your
place last Saturday but I thought I'd better phone
first. . ."

"yes, that's always best."

Winthrop says, "you ought to get an agent and a
New York publisher. Barton is fucking you."

Barton is my American editor and all the poets
he refuses to publish
tell me that he is a shit.
that shit Barton published me
when the New York publishers were

busy playing piss-in-the-hat with the dilettantes.

o.k., so well, to hell with details, it is a long
afternoon, hot, with Winthrop interjecting literary
bits and losing his tiny bets and I get to thinking
less of death rays and more of suckerfish and
I wonder why I can't just tell him to get away
from me,
to leave me some god damned solitude?
but I am a coward: I know he won't understand,
can't understand:
each one thinks they are special,
that they are different.
yet I drop enough hints, I try to nudge him off
humanely.

going into the 9th
I am $110 ahead
(I have been playing the horses for 40 years
and am only 5 grand down)
and I put $30 win on the even money shot
while Winthrop announces that he is going
to bet the 2, the 4 and the 7 and that he
feels quite sure that one of them is
going to win.
all of his horses are 20 to one or over.

my horse wins by 4 and one-half lengths,
I wave goodbye to Winthrop,
make my way to the payoff windows. . .

after 5 minutes I collect
put my money into my wallet and make
toward the stairway
and there is Winthrop walking

beside me.

down the stairway we go together
he in his polyester and knit
me in my wrinkled summer slacks and
sport shirt with cigarette holes
with the mob
walking down the stairway
they are talking horses
still holding programs and forms
tip sheets and newspapers
many old folks
creeping along slowly
barely able to walk
or understand.
it's an unholy parade,
I would as lief be elsewhere.
Winthrop and I reach the bottom of
the stairway together.
"see you," I say and turn left
toward the exit.

Winthrop is still at my elbow.
"Jesus Christ," I say, "are *you*
in valet parking too?"
"oh no," he points to the right,
"I'm over there somewhere. . ."
"well," I say, "you better get to
your car. see you. . ."
"see you," Winthrop says.

I am free.

I hand one of the parking lot attendants my
parking tab.

"black '79 BMW," I say.
"I know, champ," he says.

driving on in
with the sun roof open I
slip in a cassette of Sibelius
turn onto the San Diego freeway
south
angle right into
a monstrous traffic jam
turn up the volume of the
front and back speakers
and feel good
for the first time in
hours.

the sniveler

you're a sniveler, she said,
you snivel when she doesn't call,
I phone you and you're shit-faced on wine.

I'm a baby, I said, then too I can't figure out
how anybody can live without me.

my god, she said, you really mean that?

yes, I said.

oh my god, you're impossible, you big soft
baby's ass!

suck me off and maybe I can forget, help me
forget.

you big soft baby's ass!

I'm sensitive, yes. and how can anybody live
without me?

she hung up.

well, I thought, there's two who can live without me.
there might be 2000, 2 million, 2 billion, 2 million
billion.

it was one of the most depressing thoughts I'd had
in years.

I went into my bedroom and stretched out and looked at
the ceiling.

I thought, well, I can masturbate, I can look at television,
and then there's suicide.

having already masturbated twice that day
I had two choices left and
being a big soft baby's ass I
switched on the tv.

fear and madness

barricaded here on the 2nd floor
chair against the door
butcher knife on table
I type my first poem here
switchblade in pocket
I type this
for my tax accountant
for the girls in Omaha
for my tax accountant
for the girls in Ohio
for my tax accountant
I am broke again
I own ¼ of this house
I have a pear tree
I have a lemon tree
I have a fig tree
everybody is worried about my soul now
I am worried about my soul now
there is a balcony outside of this room
I can step out on that balcony and see the harbor
I will get drunk tonight and step out there
maybe I can fall off that balcony
and I can write about that
if I don't break my fingers and arms.

this is good no matter what they say
I have written east Hollywood to death
now I am going to write about San Pedro
I have fallen into a new arena.

"tell Chinaski welcome to suburbia,"

some body told my girlfriend
and I said, "my suburbia tells her suburbia to
go to hell."

San Pedro I will wring you out like a wet rag
San Pedro I will break you like a wild stallion
I will write about your bridge and your ships
I will skin your people down to the bone
I will make my stand here as I have made my stand elsewhere.
I will learn these walls
I will attempt to pay the mortgage
I will feed my cat
I will love my woman
I will listen to Elgar, Stravinsky and Mozart.
I will think of Henry Miller using mouth wash.
I will use all 3 bathrooms
both bedrooms
and the electric oven.

I can fail in many more ways now
I was always good at that.

the plumbing is of copper
and the typer is of me
and there's enough ground out front to live off of,
that is, if I can get my ass out of this chair.

barricaded here on the 2nd floor
I am in a small room again.

drying out

we buy the scandal sheets at the supermarket
get into bed and eat pretzels and read as outside
the churchbells ring and the dogs bark
we turn on the tv and watch very bad movies
then she goes down and brings up ice cream
and we eat the ice cream and she says,
"tomorrow night is trash night."
then the cat jumps up on the bed
drops its tongue out and stands there
glistening cross-eyed

the phone rings and it is her mother and she
talks to her mother
she hands me the phone
I tell her mother that it's too bad it's freezing
back there
it's about 85 here and,
yes, I'm feeling well and
I hope you're feeling well too

I hand the phone back

she talks some more
then hangs up

"mother is a very brave woman," she tells me
I tell her that I'm sure her mother is

the cat is still standing there glistening
cross-eyed
I push it down onto the covers

"well," she says, "we've gone two nights without
drinking."

"good," I says, "but tomorrow night I'm going to
do it."

"ah, come on," she says

"you don't have to drink," I tell her, "just because
I do."

"like hell," she says

she flips the remote control switch until she comes to a
Japanese monster movie

"I think we've seen this one," I say

"you didn't see it with me," she says, "who did you
see it with?"

"you were laying with me, right here, when we saw it,"
I tell her

"I don't think I remember this one," she says

"you just keep watching," I tell her

we keep watching
I'm not so sure anymore
but it's a peaceful night as we watch this big thing
kick the shit out of half of Tokyo.

there are hecklers in Germany too

I see you hanging from the girders
in the blue smoke of
Hamburg
hissing and hating
you writers who didn't make it
you writers who think you are great writers
you cheap shots of piss
you can't write
and everybody knows it but you
you hate and scream
why did you come
if you didn't believe in
me?
dm 10 to holler at what you
hate.
all right,
maybe it's worth it,
maybe you don't understand
but it's worth it,
you'd like to be up here
with the mike
in front of the cameras
under the tv lights,
you'd love it
that's your problem
mine is to read my stuff over your
god damned hollering.
I tell you
it's not as good as it
looks,
does that make you feel
better?

no, you don't believe
it
you cheap shots of piss
you know how to bellow
you should have been a
soprano in a Wagnerian
opera. anyhow, thanks
for the ten
dm.

just another bad affair

Paris
is the place you've heard about
it's very large and the people seem rich but very
separated from each other
each person
a temple of indifference
but
when you search these structures more intently
you see that
fear
has become a habit with them
they are stuffed with
fear
and it's the
fear
which makes them seem indifferent
to each other
and to you.

these grand Parisians,
the ladies and children
sit in the park like paper flowers
and the men roar about in their tiny cars
bravely pretending.

I'm sure the French
have done many things of import
but
it smells of the past.

to go to Paris to create art
now

would be much like sitting around
waiting for a butterfly to fart.

I like the waiters and the dogs
and the whores
and the way the people stay up
most of the night
any night
but there is a chill upon
the soul of Paris.

cities die
like people die
only more slowly
and people
who live in dying cities
become stuffed with indifference and
fear
and when their deaths
become actual
funerals seem superfluous.

Paris
you expected nothing of me
but I expected more
of you.

now that we know all this
let us quietly
say goodbye.

the American writer

gone abroad
I sit under the tv lights
and am interviewed again
I am asked questions
I give answers
I make no attempt to be
brilliant.
to be truthful
I feel bored
and I almost never feel
bored.
"do you? . . ." they ask.
"oh, yeah, well I. . ."
"and what do you think of. . ."
"I don't think of it much. I
don't think too much. . ."
somehow it ends.

that evening somebody tells me
I'm on the news
we turn the set on.
there I am. I look pissed.
I wave people off.
I *am* bored.

how marvelous to be me without
trying.
it looks on tv
as if I knew exactly what I
was doing.

fooled them
again.

Sibelius and etc.

sick on a Friday night while the discos rock of ass
and hip and leg, I'm too sick to drink,
listening to Brahms and squeezing orange
juice. when I'm too sick to drink you
know I'm sick. I didn't even buy
tomorrow's Racing Form. now there's
some Sibelius on the radio and
in the apartment house on the
corner a woman screams as a
man beats her.

there's nothing on tv. it's moments like this that
the madhouses are better understood. I've even
rolled a joint now. I found some old stuff in
the closet.
when Sibelius reached 40 he shaved
all the hair on his head, walked
into his house and never
came out again until they
came for him.

sick at the age of 57 I sit listening to
the music and smoking this poor joint
while I plan a comeback.

sick on a Friday night I understand very little. but I
like the lamplight and my cigar box keeps saying over
and over to me: *mentel charutos pimentel charutos*
pimentel charuto entel charutos pimentel charutos
pimen. . .

the woman screams again as the man
beats her. he calls her a whore.
what is he doing living with
a whore?

the woman from Germany

every 3 or 4 nights the phone rings
and it's this woman from Germany.
she keeps her calls short:
"hello," she says, "it's me."
I never ask her name.
"what are you doing?" she asks.
"drinking white wine and typing," I
say.
"you always say that."
"that means that things are good."
"I've had some red wine. how are things with
you?"
"more bad affairs," I say, "they all end up
badly."
"mine too," she answers.
"it's sad, isn't it? I want to quit."
"I can't quit," she answers.
"good. I don't think I can either."
"I'm going to sleep now. goodnight."
"goodnight," I say.

and I can see her in her bedroom. I can see her
put the phone down. now she puts out the light.
she pulls the covers up, inhales and exhales deeply.
she is sad. her walls cover her. she is alone.
I want to know her name.

parked

sitting in my car
on Catalina Avenue in Redondo Beach
I see a fellow of 19 or 20
riding his bicycle on the sidewalk.
he wears sandals and blue shorts,
slows down, stops, puts one foot down,
sits upon his bicycle seat.
it is 4:30 in the afternoon and
he is tanned a deep and even tan,
has yellow hair and mustache.
his face is smooth
unmarked by pain or experience.
then something animates him
and he pedals off.

another crosses the street,
he must be 21,
very large of chest, blond,
blue-eyed, very tanned, wearing
green shorts and sandals.
it is a Tuesday afternoon.
he stands a moment
looking down the street.
his face is the same as the
other face:
without expression or purpose.
a long cigarette is in his mouth.
he finally enters a liquor store,
comes out a moment later
holding a can of Bubble-Up.

these are the kind that my parents wanted

me to be
the kind my country wanted me to
be
the kind the girls wanted me to
be.

I start the engine and back out of
there
thinking about
Leo Durocher, Machine Gun Kelly,
Rocky Marciano, Two Ton Tony Galento
and Dutch Van Gogh.

at Vegas you have to put up two to get one

typing in a room full of smoke
getting up
opening the door
going to the bathroom to piss
coming back
filling the glass
lighting a cigarette
typing again
poem number 6
poem number 7
getting drunker
what a floor show
a run of bombers murdering the natives
and the elephants
blasting huts and trees into storms of fire,
sitting in my shorts
balls hanging out of shorts,
finding wristwatch face-down in ashtray,
turning it,
looking:
only one-thirty a.m.,
time for another run
this time to blow away the whores of
rhyming poets,
first gotta piss once more
change the radio station
holler down the stairway to the woman:
"hey, baby, you all right?"

dummy

we've lived together 3 or
4 years and I'm 23 years older than
she.

she takes me into the bathroom:
"look here. look at this. you've
made peepee on the floor again!"

"ah, come on. . ."

"admit it! you did it. . . !"

some time later she shows me
a bedsheet: "look, see that dark
mark? that's where you sat down!
that's *shit*! don't you wipe your
behind?"

"yeah. . ."

"I don't think you do. . ."

when I drive the car she says:
"what are you doing? you're going
in the wrong direction! and I don't
want to correct you, I *know* how much
that upsets you . . . but now you're
driving in second gear and you
should be driving in first! that's
not good for your car!"

when I stand in the bathroom shaving or

just looking at my face and wondering,
she come in, grabs a deodorant stick
and begins rubbing it under my arms,
around my buttocks, behind my
neck.

"we want you to smell good. . . remember
when I saw peanuts coming out of your
ass in bed? how do you explain that?"

"I told you how that happened. . ."

"no, no, the peanuts were coming out
of your ass! how are you doing, peanut-
ass?"

"not so good, I guess. . ."

"why don't you put the soap back in
the soap dish?"

"all right. . ."

*

when I first met her she said,
"you are my sage!"

but like I said that was 3 or
4 years ago.
and I always told her,
"I'm no sage."

now that's settled.

virgins

sitting in this little Mexican bar in San Pedro
Sunday afternoon, 5:30 p.m.
the walls are decorated with Indians in head dress
carrying virgins to sacrifice.
where did they find all these virgins?

the young man from the bar brings me another beer.
he is a nice boy, kind and caring, possibly
homosexual.

"how are you feeling?" he asks. "not so good,"
I say. "how so?" he asks.
I tap my head and smile: "it's the mind. . ."
"oh," he says. "it's nothing," I say,
"a few more drinks will cure it. . ."
"you drink," he says, "like a very thirsty man."
"I am," I say.

it's on afternoons like this that I should be
at the racetrack connecting with a $312 exacta.
not that the money matters
it's just nice to see something working right for a
moment
like a boa constrictor, like a tiger, like a paper clip.

there are new virgins this early evening
exploding across the surface
of the wall
crawling into the fireplaces
and coming out of my ears riding great white
horses
as I rise from the table with my shameful

gut
the Mexican beer backed up like a
swamp of unsatisfactory days and
nights
I make it to the parking lot
let it go between two brilliantly waxed low-
riders in the moonlight.

now there's room for whiskey.

let nothing ever happen

I drove in for gas and began filling my tank
and the attendant was a fat man dressed all in
orange.
he stood there watching and I had this feeling
that I should take the gas nozzle
jam it into his mouth
and fill him with about
five gallons of supreme.

I filled the tank instead
and hung up the hose.

I paid
got my change
and he watched me as I walked to the
front of my car
kicked the right front tire hard
circled the car
got in
and drove off.

I drove north down Pacific Coast Highway and it was all
right until I came to these orange
road-markers
which narrowed the three lanes down
to one.
traffic slowed
then stopped in a long line
for a red signal.
they had us all in the left
lane.

I looked out the right window
and saw this blond road-worker with a
beard.

he tossed a road-marker through the air
to another road-worker with a beard.
he caught it
laughed and tossed it back.
they were playing catch.

hell, I remember when only hermits wore
beards.

the lane to the left wasn't moving and
I wanted to make a right turn
and there was nothing going on in the
other lanes
but this game of catch.

I cut into the right lane.
the blond boy saw me coming and
missed his catch.
as I drove past him he screamed,
"what the hell are you doing?"

I stopped my car and got out.
as I walked up to the blond the other
worker ran up.
he stopped in front of me.
"you can't drive in this lane,"
he said.

"what the hell are you doing?" asked
the blond.

"if a cop was around he'd tag your
ass!" said the other boy.

"are you a cop?" I asked.

"no, you can see I'm not a cop."

"this is what the hell I am doing: I'm going to get into
my car and make a right turn from this lane."

"who the fuck do you think you are?" asked the
blond.

"I don't know who I am, but I'm going to get into
my car now and make a right turn from this lane."

"yeah," said the other boy, "you can eat shit too!"

"there's too much of it around here, I'm going to leave you
with it."

I got into my car
started it and
made my right turn.

I shouldn't have done that, I thought.
it's when you do things like that too often that
they put you in the madhouse.
maybe it's happening: this thing I've been
fighting against
so long.

I thought about driving back and
apologizing: "listen, fellows, I know I was wrong
and I've come back here to ask your forgiveness."

or I could go back to the gas station man:
"listen, do you know that I was thinking of filling
you with five gallons of supreme and I'm here to
apologize for that."

but I just kept driving along.
if I was careful I could hide among all of them
for years.
as I stopped for a signal there were cars all
around me.
I turned my radio on loud
to the worst music I could
find.

the vampires

I am hungover and in bed and the doorbell rings.
it is eleven a.m.
"what the *shit*?" I ask.
she goes to the door and I hear her talking.
she enters the bedroom and tells me,
"it's a Mr. Sanderson," she says, "he says you
know him and he wants to talk to you."
"Sanderson?" I ask, "what's his first name?"
she comes back with the answer: "he says his
first name is Frank."
"never heard of the son of a bitch. tell him
to get the hell out of here."
I hear them talking back and forth and
I consider all that very unnecessary and
I begin to get up and get dressed
to run him off.
when I get there he is gone.
"what did he want?" I ask.
"he wanted to talk to you," she says.
"well now, isn't that the cat's tit?"
"he looked like a very nice boy, he looked very sad
when you sent him off."
"I don't want to talk to any son of a bitch,"
I tell her.
"well, I would have talked to him," she says.

that night I am on my 4th or 5th beer when
there is a brutal knocking upon the door.
I figure murder, emergency, anything. . .
somebody needs help. . .
I open the door.
it is a fat son of a bitch and

behind him are 5 or 6 other people
male and female.
"HEY!" screams the fat man, "I'M BO SEAVERS AND
       WE'VE COME TO
SAY HELLO!"
I swing the door shut but he sticks a big shoe in there
holding it open.
"hold it," he says, "we're a lot alike, you'll really dig
me. many people mistake me for you."
"get your god damned foot out of the jamb," I say.
I take the heel of my shoe and crush it down
on his toes.
the foot withdraws and I slam the door.
—after a moment beer cans and bottles hit against
the door, then a rock or two.
I hear some curses and then I hear them
walking off.

I sit down and open a new beer.
"ever since I was about 16," I tell her,
"people have been after me and it has never
stopped: 44 years worth of that.
I don't know what they want with me because,
you see, I most certainly dislike them."

"maybe if you'd just give them a chance,"
she says, "you'll find that everybody is an
individual if you'll just search them
out."

I drain my beer on that one,
then look at her:
"how the fuck did *you* get in here?"

I walk into the kitchen and find the
scotch, unpeel it and pour a hit as

the phone rings.
I hear her answer:
"who? I'll ask him. . ."

I hear her walking toward me
in the kitchen
and I wonder why she doesn't already
know the answer
as I stand there holding the drink
watching the faucet leak
the way they do.

produced and bottled by. . .

bleakly wandering flat white fields
listening for the sound of engines
my love is gone out another night.
she has needs. "you," she says,
"hate people. I like them. . ."
she needs fresh air.
I feed the cats, bathe myself,
watch the telly.
she's stuck on this guy, died in 1969,
claimed he was God, came from
India, hung around Hollywood.
there is a photo of him in the bathroom
we look at each other while I crap.

I begin thinking of old girlfriends
or of finding new ones
but that's so much work
and you get one
and she lasts for ten or fifteen
months
then skitters off into some new kind
of insanity.

and then too
you get to thinking
maybe it's yourself.
I certainly wouldn't like to
sit around with me
night after night. . .

but one thing about drinking
about the bottle

it might kill you
but it will kill you
with faithfulness
and sitting here with these
3 cats and this 1976 bottle
of Napa Valley red
I have to tell you,
faithfulness,
that's something rare.

retreat

well
if you didn't call for an enema
this is the A train to Norwalk,
and
the troops
will be brisking through here
soon
and you know
they ain't going to
leave the tits on a rat.

Thompson killed himself
last night
in his shining brass room
he drank silver paint
until his belly
came
out of his eyes.

remember the rule:
everything starts over at
each moment
and all that's past
is more useless
than what is
present.

we've raped
all the girls
40 times over.
we've left nothing

for the enemy except
the residue
of our cowardice.

no matter. . .
cowardice is the aftermath
of imagination.

shit, it's cold, though
you know
I imagine
death is not so bad
if the temperature
is decent.

but pain wearies me
it goes
on and on.
I think I've found
little methods
to escape it
and then it
shows me
the same thing
in a different
form.

hell,
I talk too much
we should
really
move out.
I see the flares
dropping now.
there's no use

having another
meeting
of minds
there's nothing
left to solve.
the victorious
are getting ready
to arrive
and we've been
caught
out of place.

can't we
take back
move #45
and substitute
move #39?
that's the one
we should have
made.

well
let's go
give me your arm. . .
oh, it's
gone . . . you
motherfucker. . .

you know
I can't believe
we've lost.
it didn't take
any effort
at all.
I guess the

worst and best
things don't—
which leaves
the in
between and that
qualifies too.

careful,
the steps are
covered with
ice. . .
I really like
your falcon tattoo. . .

I don't know
where we're going
but
isn't it better
than having them
catch you
with your hand
around your
pecker?

let's sing
something,
huh?
how about a
love song?
I wish I knew
a hate song. . .

you know
I was
eleven years old

before I could whistle?

watch your
head
we're coming
out
and don't worry
I heard a
story once
that being killed
is the same as
killing. . .

so all we have
to do
now
is
to
walk out of
here. . .

the embracers

I always meet these gregarious
females
who attend class at
night:
sculpting, ballet, acting and
etc.
and who are understanding
who embrace art and humanity
in almost all of its
shapes.

their phones are busy for
hours
their monthly phone bills are
unbelievable
they are chatting with new
girlfriends or old boyfriends
in Duluth, Pittsburgh and New Haven
or mothers and sisters in
Miami and Sacramento.

while I am at their place
an old boyfriend arrives
just a *friend*
and he sits on the rug
for a good stay and a
chat.

well, he used to be
homosexual
went straight

used to be a
drunkard
quit
used to take acid
speed and etc.
now clean
now going to get
married
now all right
and chitting and
jibbering away about
it
like a chimpanzee
like a hot nozzle douche.
we're invited to the
wedding and to a small
party afterwards
the real reception will
be a week after that
he's a gourmet
cook and it takes days to
prepare the food
and so it would be better
not to have *that*
reception right after the
wedding. he doesn't belong
to the same therapy group as
his future wife
she's into Scientology
but if people really *care,*
fuck it, you know, they'd
both been through
plenty and they'd work it
out. and, and, and, and,
and, and.

he leaves and I am told,
"that was Rodney, I've known
him for ten years. his father
died a few months ago and he
had to take over the family business.
it was a strain on him. I
don't think you've met his
girlfriend. she left her
piano at my place once and
there was kind of a mess
over that but I think she's
good for him. . ."

I don't know what to say
to these gregarious women.
I lost my enthusiasm for
the masses at the age
of 4.

the cats too

your niece came and left
and your mother came and left
I outlived their problems
next I will rip up the cornstalks
in the garden,
maybe we can burn them in the fireplace, ears and all, I have never
burned ears, have you?

the old folks next door are gone.
are they dead or visiting in
Kansas? when they die, you know
who's next? everybody. the
cats too, the cats too.

death or no, it's still nice to
live in the same place for two or
three years, no landlord banging.
one can get drunk and break the
windows, puke anywhere; one can
sing, scream, roll down the
stairway; one can step out on the
balcony and see all the way to
Long Beach.

it's all very literary.

the movie people come by, the
interviewers, the translators, the
editors, the publishers, the
suckerfish; we get them all drunk,
we get much drunker than they and

we talk for hours, smoking our cigars,
swallowing their pills, smoking *their*
stuff, we talk until sunrise,
into the morning, pouring more drinks, coming out
of the kitchen with ever-new bottles, pulling out
the corks; I am two or three times their age; they
nod sleepily, they don't want to hear any more,
they wanted to hear about *creation,* how it's done;
I never talk about that, it doesn't interest me, it
doesn't mean anything, only talking about playing
the horses means something, you see, it all revolves
around the horses, that's the secret, you want the
secret? that's the secret. . .

oh? oh, yes, is . . . that it?

they leave.

I wear them down. I make them hate. I give them
more than they want. they want to suck blood, I give
them pus. they leave.

they want to know, where can I get my stuff published,
some of them want to know that. and if you suggest a
place, they send their work with a note: "Chinaski
suggested that I send this to you. . ."

it's all very literary.

if I, with this minor fame, am gutted with them what
does Truman Capote do?

here where the refrigerator works and the toilet
flushes and no Hindus prowl
the best way to forget the past is to live in the present
as if we deserved it, though we worry about the luck

and also shell-shock and the brain-damaged de-
ranged past. . . Children, have you read Alex Comfort,
Christopher Morley and Conrad Aiken?

anyhow, no landlord banging here now
one cat asleep in the car, another half-asleep
stuffed with horsemeat on top of the tv set
and the third out front being fractional with
the possums who live in the hedge.

my tax accountant phoned today and said not to
worry, he'd write the tax people in Frankfurt
and tell them that under the Double
Taxation Convention with the USA that I have
already sacrificed the runner to second.

where was this guy when I was trying to sleep
on that park bench in El Paso during the 1941
sandstorm? while half the world was burning?

it's 2:15 a.m. and you aren't drinking, I've
drunk almost all of it myself and there are two
bottles of beer left.
you are downstairs watching a space program
on tv and I won $147 at the track today,
clean line zinging here, only one landlord can
knock now—that mouldy parasite, he'll finally
collect
here where the succotash is fine and murder
episodes flower on our tv
I'll sleep soon after drinking those two
bottles of beer
I've finished writing this
it's literary history.

guava tree

I lay with my white belly up to the sun under the pineapple
guava tree while other people's children are at school
any my woman is at work and it is quiet and I am alone with the
birds and I count eleven of them on the wire overhead
and there's nothing to do here.
before there was always much for me to do
but it was always the other man's idea
the other man who was making all the money using me
and also the foreman he hired to cause me trouble
we were pitted against each other and that just wasn't
sensible because he was almost as poor as I, it was
tiring and deathly like something sucking at
your blood.
well, I wasn't a revolutionary, I only wanted to save
my own ass, I figured that would be easier than saving
humanity's ass. . .

now under the pineapple guava tree I am still sucking at
the free hours
I can never suck enough free hours, blinking at the
sun, scratching my nose, nowhere to go and nothing to do
glorious
the boys would never guess how I did it and I hardly know
     myself
but I knew in the factories, I knew in those places that
I wanted out, my eye always on the window, the doorway,
and the workers liked me because they thought I was crazy
and the foremen were puzzled because I worked hard
but with disdain.

now under the pineapple guava tree, the sun cutting through
the branches, I still have the body of a young boy

but the face is old
remembering the hours and the places and what was done
to the days and the weeks and the years.

I turn on my belly, spread both arms wide feeling like
the wolf who got out of the trap but without gnawing a
leg away.
they got something, of course, that's why I'm still
resting, but it's the parts that are left that I'm
celebrating under this pineapple guava tree just
before noon.

ng my money's worth

the water was cold and filled with bits of seaweed
it looked strangely like little pieces of broken shit
and nobody went into the water
and I told her,
"I'm gong in. we drove one hundred and seventy miles
to get here and we are paying $30 a night for a motel room
with a shower stall built for people 4 feet tall. I'm
going in."
"not me," she said.
I left her on her STAR WARS towel
I entered the water
small hard rocks underfoot
I walked in chilled
reaching down and splashing myself.
then the first wave came and I dove under
I could feel the seaweed clinging to me
it had been a great hurricane
the best of the year
as I stood up an unbroken mass of seaweed wound
around me.
I broke from the tendrils
turned and waved to her on the shore
beckoning—
"come on in, chickenshit. . ."
I turned in time to dive under the new
breaker
then I swam for ten or fifteen yards
parallel to the shore.
I turned again and waved her in—
"come on, show some guts!"
she waved me off—
"go on, be an asshole! not me!"

I leaped high
breaking through and over the next wave.
Del Mar was a fine place
even though the racetrack was unlucky for me.
as I settled down upon the ocean bottom
my left foot stepped on something soft
which appeared to be alive.
I leaped away
falling backwards into the water
and the next wave passed over me.
I rolled over and was carried toward the shore.
I got up and walked through the broken seaweed
pulling my trunks up.
I walked over the rocks and onto the shore
then up on the sand.
"you didn't stay very long," she said.
"I stepped on something out there, it was
alive. I got the fuck out."
"dry off and lay down," she said.
"I'm going to shower. I've got to make the first
race."
"o.k.," she said, "I'll see you about the 5th.
I want to get some sun."

I walked back to the motel and got under the
4-foot shower. what had I stepped on? a dead
fish? an eel?
I got out and dried off, selected my short-
sleeved blue shirt
tan pants
loafers
green bikini underwear.

the good life of the California
sportsman.

guest

we got drunk
and then he started,
he said, listen, I know that
people claim you're uneducated
and unread
but here we've been talking about
The Red and the Black.
you know that Lorca was gunned down
in a Spanish road.
you've mentioned many painters
and I know that you know
the great musicians.
you know who wrote *The Cherry
Orchard.*
you know that Ambrose Bierce was
killed by Mexican bandits.
and you know who wrote *The Devil's
Dictionary.*
you know who whipped Hemingway's
ass and that Gertrude Stein had a
wooden leg.
you know of the one who went mad
in a rowboat.
you know who died of syphilis.
and you know that Anton Chekov
shot his dog. pardon me. . .

he got up, went into the bathroom.
I could hear him puking.

then he walked out, sat on the couch,
lit his pipe, took a hit on his beer
can, put it down and passed out quietly,

sitting there, his head dropping
just a bit.

she came down the stairway.
is he all right?

he's all right. he's staying
tonight, I think.

I'm sorry I left but I couldn't
listen anymore, he just kept
talking.

it's all right, I said.

I turned off the lights and went up the
stairway with her.

it's pitiful, she said, he *adores*
you.

he thinks I'm a genius, I
said.

are you? she asked as we got to
the bedroom.

I will be if I can get rid of
him.

we stood there getting undressed.

have you brushed your teeth?
she asked.

many times, I answered.

then I got into bed, fast.
I was better at getting into bed
than anybody that I knew.

then she climbed in:
is your friend downstairs going to
be all right?

he'll make it through the night and he'll
return, I told her.

some things you sleep away.
and I decided to do just that and
as we faced away
I moved my feet to the backs
of her calves
while half a block down
the dogs of night
barked about nothing.

war

the black and the yellow met
at the bottom of the hill.
the black stopped dead by the crash
and the yellow veering away from the
black
and coming directly at me with
the driver slumped over the wheel.
I should put my car in reverse,
I thought, but my hand didn't move
on the gearshift.
then the yellow slanted off
and I thought, it's not going to hit
me squarely, it's going to scrape the
side; and then it passed my right side
silently,
you couldn't have slipped a sheet of paper
between us.
then the yellow crashed head-on into the
car of a man braked to my right two
car lengths back.
the yellow pushed him back, bounced off,
slanted crazily behind my car, crossed the
street, ran into a curbing and was still.

I had not seen the initial crash
I had only heard it.
I circled into a gas station
and sat there
looking at the three crushed silent cars.

if I had put it in reverse,
I would have been there too.
I started the engine and drove

out thinking, let's see? where was I
going. oh yes, the post office.
I need stamps.

I hit the classical music button
on the car radio.

table for two

it was down at the waterfront and we
waited at the bar for a table.

they sure don't make bartenders like
they used to make them
this one looked like a piece of silk
tacked over a doorway leading
nowhere.

he kept leaning toward a girl at the
bar.
the girl was built like a machine gun
tower out of World War I.
she spit some tracer bullets out of
her mouth:
"you ain't gettin' my fuckin' pussy
you snake-brained turd!"

it was then that the bartender noticed
us staring
behind the bar at
the many lovely bottles.
so he came over and said, "good
evening," and we ordered and he
walked off with his tiny precious
Mick Jagger ass.

my girlfriend looked out at the harbor
view: "look at those boats out there,"
she said. "I wish we had a boat."
"yeah," I said.

the bartender sliced back into view.

I noticed the tiny seaweed earring in
his left ear as he proceeded to set the
drinks down sloshing away
one-fourth of each.
then he reached for a dirty rag and
wiped the dry area around the edges
of the puddles.
"that bitch down there," he nodded toward
her, "she thinks she's hot shit!"
I told him, "I think she looks like a
machine gun tower out of World War I."
the bartender said, "oh, that's *good*!
I'm going to tell her that!"

so he walked down and told the lady
and she turned and looked at me.
she said, "hey, buddy! fuck you!"
I nodded my head at her
not quite knowing why.

"hey," said my girlfriend, "are you
coming on to her?"

"no," I
said.

"god damn," she said, "sometimes I
think you're just some kind of fuck-
twist!"

"what do you mean by that?" I asked.

"oh shit," she said, "forget it."

I motioned for a couple more drinks.
the bartender came on down.

"I told her what you said," he
said.

"we'll have two more," I
told him.

"what were they?" he asked.

"check the puddles," I pointed to
the bar, "we'll have the same."

the woman down at the bar looked
at me again: "fuck you, buddy!"

I got up and found the men's
room.
as I stood at the urinal
gagging and pissing
a crapper door opened and a
midget walked out.
he took an orange tennis ball
out of his pocket.
he cocked his arm and threw a
line drive at the mirror.
the mirror didn't break.
and as the ball zipped back
he leaped into the air and caught
it in his mouth.
then, while holding the ball in
his mouth
he did a little tap dance like
Fred Astaire and
was gone.

I walked back to the bar and sat
down next to my girlfriend:

"I don't want to eat here. let's
go."

"but the view's great!" she said.
"we can sit at a table and watch the
boats going in and out."

I threw some bills down on the
bar.
"no, let's go, to hell with it."

"nothing ever quite works for
you, does it?" she asked.

"no," I answered.

I got up and she followed me.

as we passed the lady at the
bar she said, "fuck you, buddy!"

I was about to open the door
when somebody pushed the door from
the outside.
the door opened in and I threw
up my forearm as the door slammed
into it.
the man who had opened the door had
a head like a pumpkin and he was with
a woman whose face looked like a seal's
face and she had on a little hat
only the little hat looked like a large
wristwatch had been fastened to the top of it.

"oh," said the man, "terribly sorry!"

as we walked into the night the man
held the door open and the lady with the
wristwatch on her hat kept looking at
me as if she couldn't believe that the door
had actually hit me on the
forearm.

we walked out into the parking lot and
suddenly
I don't know why
I had to piss again and I unzipped and
stood between two cars
one was black and large and the other was
green and medium-sized.
I decided to let it go on the green
one.

"someday you are going to get caught
doing that," said my girlfriend.

"oh yes," I said, "I'm sure that I
will."

let it go

pissing drunk
   in the middle of the night
      on the second floor of somewhere
symphony music on—
   quite a good boy working out.

it's good to have the arts
   to let it go on.

I flush.
   shake it.
      wash my hands.

the symphony music is exceptional—
   large emotional cartwheels
      of glory.

it's good to have the arts
   to let it go on.

suppose we didn't have that
   to let it go on?
we'd jump off buildings or
   murder our lovers.

I go naked down the stairway.
   she is there watching an old movie on tv.

"you ought to put something on,"
   she says,
      "you'll catch cold."

you see, it's nice that we have

somebody who doesn't want us
    to get sick,
and also after pissing in the
    middle of the night it's nice
        to be recognized.

"how long you going to stay up?"
    you ask her.

"this thing is terrible," she says,
    "but I have to find out
        how it ends."

I go into the kitchen
    open the refrigerator and
        stare inside.
I don't know what I want there
    somehow it looks more like a
        clothes closet.

I close the refrigerator door
    admire the fat click
        it makes
then I go to the stairway
    walk up.

pissing
    can be
        quite an
adventure.

notes upon a hot streak:

I have been driving to the racetrack
for thirty years now
in some of the worst junk cars
imaginable.
I have outlived most of the parking lot
attendants
but now as I drive up in a new BMW
some of them remember me from the
old days
"hey, champ," they say, *"how's it
going?"*
"it's going good," I tell them.
"got a good one for me, champ?"
they ask
I wink and drive on in.

they think I am making it at the
races, they think I have solved the
ponies.

*"hey, champ, who was that young girl
you were with the other day?"*

I drive on in.

I play the horses like other men
play chess:
make the proper moves and make
them well.
and lately, after all these years,
I have begun to win and I leave
with little bundles of money each
day.

it's a very odd feeling
but I accept it,
use valet parking
to the clubhouse.

it is a lovable comedy:
both the writing and the
betting:
they are letting me win
for this moment.

but the attendants seem to think
that I know some secret:
*"you're looking good, champ,
just give me one good one and
I won't bother you anymore!"*

I smile and drive on in.

do you use a notebook?

many a time when I drive this black beauty out of the driveway
of my home, drive down the hill, turn right at the signal,
wait, take a left, run down 3 blocks take another left, go
another 2 blocks and I'm onto the freeway
many a time I think,
what am I doing here?
why am I in this car?
where am I supposed to be?—
going to the racetrack at 11 a.m. while other men are working
I turn on the radio and light a cigarette.
what am I doing with this leisure?
where did the factories go?
and the whores?
and the drunktanks?

then
such thoughts pass
and I begin to think about my new system, it's going quite
well—it's most interesting how just 3 numbers
balanced against each horse selects the winner about
40% of the time.

. . . and then the thoughts mix as I cut between a tanker and
a Volks: when the interviewers come by they want to know
about writing—
what are your influences?
do you use a notebook?
do you revise?
why do you write?

. . . and I begin talking about the horses and my system and
everybody looks discouraged, including the lady I live with.

"he always talks like this," she tells them.

*

I drive the black beauty toward the track, opening the
automatic roof for more sunshine.

they don't understand—it's been a gamble all along;
nothing ever solidifies into a sure thing; all gifts
must constantly be earned and re-earned; also, to linger
incessantly upon the ground of literature and learning
is not only inhuman, it's dumb.

. . . driving into the track I stop to pay the parking lot
attendant.
he knows me: "how's it going, champ?"
"just trying to make it," I tell him.

I drive toward preferred parking, valet's no good:
they burn the cold engines out returning the machines to
the people after the 9th race.

I park between a Dodge van and a Volks Rabbit
thinking, Ernie would have understood and surely,
Manolete, and certainly all the people here ahead of me,
already parked and in there waiting, getting
ready.

I step out, lock the car and walk toward the gate,
it is a meaningful and beautiful day, and knowing
the terror, the luck and the grace, I move
deliberately toward the action,
the mountains up there like that
listening to my footsteps as I walk on in.

smooth

slowly driving the back streets of the town, looking at
old houses, garbage cans, fences . . . in decay;
driving through the warehouse district,
then running the car down to the harbor, parking,
getting out, getting a coffee at a stand,
then sitting at a table watching ships as long as
a city block going out to sea, thinking of all the women
now gone and how important each one had seemed
of enormous importance
an importance bigger than any of the ships
and now they were elsewhere with other men
or alone.
getting up, back to the car, driving to the market
to get oranges and wine, radishes, green onions, toilet
paper,
looking at the people who had once seemed so dangerous,
now they were listless, pushing their carts,
no arguments, no trouble, no impatience.
even the racetracks were closed because of a special
holiday.
getting into the car with the goods
driving the back streets
there are children playing some game,
they step back to let the car through;
no curses, no rocks thrown, silence,
afternoon into evening, an effortless evolving;
no ambulances, not even a dead dog in the street.

it's going to be a bad night,
I'm going to be mean to my woman and it's not going to be
her fault.

message

I've been sitting in this
room for hours
typing, and drinking
red wine.

I thought I was
alone here.
the door is closed and
the window.

now a big fat fly
ugly and black
sits on the edge
of my wine glass.

where did it come
from?
so silent, motionless
like that.

that's the way
it might be
with death.

they ruin your day

I parked the BMW and went in to get some papers
xeroxed.
I watched the white sheets of paper jump out of
the machine.
it was a warm and easy day.
I clipped the papers together
paid the clerk and walked out on the street again.

and here he came in seaman's cap
blue work shirt and pants rolled too high.

there were others but he walked right up to me
grabbed my hand and began shaking it:
"hey, buddy, urgworg buddy lapu ssot udorob
I am your brother sag llah worg . . ."

"you're breaking my hand," I told
him.

I reached into my pocket and gave him a
quarter.

"wrogssarg buddy ssamniknat, you yremaerc . . ."
I walked on but he shouted after me: "ecin
wolley yemttrid ereth . . ."

I never liked such situations because I felt like
a fool if I gave up the money and I felt like a
bastard if I didn't.
and no matter what I did or didn't do
it just didn't go away for a while.

I walked to my car
unlocked it
got in and sat there.
some girls were coming out of a cafe after lunch.
they were going back to work
a whole group of them chatting and walking along
and I stared hard at their breasts and their legs
and their behinds
but it didn't help.

I started the car and drove down 6th to Pacific.
I crossed Pacific and went all the way to Gaffey
and it wasn't until I turned off Gaffey and
on to 3rd and saw a boy on a lawn holding a dog
while another boy strangled the dog with a rubber
hose
that I forgot about that bum at all.

der

I've cleaned this room up
entirely
everything is up off the
floor
I even washed the top of this
desk

all is in order
now

paper clips
there
dictionary
here

stapler over to the
left
radio against the
wall
ashtray cleaned
out

stamps and international coupons in cigar
box

proper month showing on
calendar

unanswered letters in middle
drawer

3 corkscrews in a
dish

all is in order
now

the garbage in this room filled an
entire trash can

I look about
all this space
this cleanliness

it's nice
here

but I can't
write
I can't
write
I CAN'T
WRITE

and I think of Lenny
Bruce's immortal line:
I CAN'T
COME

now I sit in this
place
and
I can't
write
and
I can't
come
either.

my big fling

it was a bad night
one of those
where all the talk
only makes it worse,
uglier and uglier.
I was never one
who cared much for
"discussion"
anyhow
so I slammed the
door
got into my car
and then I was
on the freeway
radio on
driving north
into the big town.
I still knew a
few girls
from the past.

I got a motel room
on Sunset Boulevard
opened the bottle
had a drink
undressed
took a shower
came out
turned on the black
and white tv
laid on the bed
and had another drink.

then something came to
me,
I knew that any woman
an old girl friend
or a new one
only meant more of
what I had just gotten away
from.

I didn't turn on the
lights, it felt good
in that dark room,
it was quiet, far away
from war
of any sort.

I stayed on the bed
and watched tv.
I had never cared much
for tv
but watching
all those people
with all their desires
and all their troubles
amused me.

I watched and I had
two bottles and I finished
one and I started the other
and I watched tv.
I felt like a boy who had
run away from home and
had found
his first room.

when the second bottle was

emptied
I slept.

when I got back
at noon
the next day
I didn't expect her
to ask me if I had been
fucked
and she didn't.
also, I didn't ask
her and I didn't care.

she was quiet.
the screaming was
over.

and two or three days
later
talking easily about
it
we found out
we had watched the same
tv programs,
the only thing was
she said she didn't like
them
and I said
I did.

and we left it
like that.

contemporary literature, one

I got drunk once and told
her about it.
how I had lived in a
paper shack in Atlanta
$1.25 a week rent
no light
no water
no toilet
no heat

nothing in my
pockets
not even a
penny

it was freezing

no friends

parents 3,000
miles away
who refused to
send money

only a six-page
letter from my
father
reminding me of
my failures
of my refusal
to face
reality

of my stupidity
for wanting to
be a writer.

all my manuscripts
returned from the
magazines

once weighing
198 pounds I now
weighed 133

there was a wire
which dangled over-
head
a wire which had
once fed a
lightbulb

I reached for that
wire
not knowing
whether it was alive
or dead

I waved my hand
near it
closer and
closer

then I stopped

I saw some newspapers
on the floor

I was out of writing

paper
had long ago hocked
my typewriter

I noticed that
each page of the
newspaper had a wide white
margin around the
edge

I had a pencil
stub

I picked up a
newspaper and with
the pencil stub
I began to write
words
on the edge

sitting in the doorway
freezing in the moonlight
so that I could
see
I wrote in pencil
on all the edges
of all the newspapers
in that shack.

*

I got drunk
one night
and told her
about that shack

263

again

and she said,
"I've heard that
story before."

then she climbed into
the new $10,000 Fiat
I had given her
for her birthday
and drove down to
the corner
market
to shop for our
dinner
that night.

the film makers

I can't shoot pool, don't want
to, am told by people I know
that certain movies are great,
and I attend these movies
feeling low-
down
sitting there in a seat
among the lonely and
insufficient people,
and the screen flashes
its genius
only it's not there
it misses as it has
almost always missed —
millions of dollars
pissed away.
the people are so used
to being conned
they get gross mixed up
with great.

it's easy to bitch, I
guess most do
about the wrong things.
but about the movies
I can't help saying
now and then,
why don't you stop
this?

but maybe *they* don't
even know.

maybe the creators of films
and the public are
alike.

I don't even want
to go on
about it.
it's raining tonight
and I've just opened the door
and spots of wet
are coming in,
probably
radioactive.

when I was a boy
we used to play
King of the Hill.

"hey, I'm King of
the Hill! Come get
me!"

now there isn't even
a hill.

the other night
this Italian film crew
came around.
"hey, look we got an
idea. we'll film you
shooting a game of
pool in some
dive!"

I told them to get

their cameras out
and to go along
with them.

in this palace —
the earth —
pigs shit in
golden bathrooms
and the deaths
of fools
are followed by
motorcades
six blocks long.

I've closed the
door
now.
the rain is
no longer coming
in.

the bastards
left behind
a piece of
equipment.
which means that
they'll be
back.

people who hang around
celluloid
usually
are.

slow night

the
*Côte de Nuits-Villages Louis
Jadot* is gone
but there is
some *San Martin Petite Sirah*
1976.
now that was a hell of a year
wasn't it?
but 1936 and 1926
1946 and 1956
weren't much.

1980?
I sit in a room
conscious of my elbows
and my wrists
typing naked at
11:17 p.m.

my father's big ugly flapping
ears have been dead for some
time now.
he used to beat me with that unbelievable razor strop
three or four times a week
in the bathroom also used to
shit in, shave in, bathe in.

my father was created by
forces he couldn't defeat;
he even failed to break me,
and you know how that must have made him
feel;

the poor fellow became
unhappier and unhappier,
his unhappiness grew narrow
while my misery grew
immense.

tonight I think of him,
February 5, 1980,
how I gave it up
surrendered to the magic of
the word—
no woman as beautiful,
no greater wealth:
without knowing what he did
my father moulded whatever
artist there is in
me.

it's time to stop,
too much red wine,
cigarette ash upon the white belly
nicotine-browned fingers typing
I am grinning
I am a religion with a new god
my father has been dead for
some time
and you are what is
killing me
now.

the secret of my endurance

I still get letters in the mail, mostly from cracked-up
men in tiny rooms with factory jobs or no jobs who are
living with whores or no woman at all, no hope, just
booze and madness.
Most of their letters are on lined paper
written with an unsharpened pencil
or in ink
in tiny handwriting that slants to the
left
and the paper is often torn
usually halfway up the middle
and they say they like my stuff,
I've written from where it's at, and
they recognize that. truly, I've given them a second
chance, some recognition of where they're at.

it's true, I was there, worse off than most
of them.
but I wonder if they realize where their letters
arrive?
well, they are dropped into a box
behind a six-foot hedge with a long driveway leading
to a two car garage, rose garden, fruit trees,
animals, a beautiful woman, mortgage about half
paid after a year, a new car,
fireplace and a green rug two-inches thick
with a young boy to write my stuff now,
I keep him in a ten-foot cage with a
typewriter, feed him whiskey and raw whores,
belt him pretty good three or four times
a week.
I'm 59 years old now and the critics say
my stuff is getting better than ever.

too late

about to walk into a supermarket today
here came an old woman dressed in floppy
white, must have been sixty-eight, knobby
knees, tits all gone, hair shot to hell in the
wind, she had something in mind, banging
along with her shopping cart full of
sundries, she arched her brows together
tightly above her nose and drove her
gondola of goodies right into me *hard,*
the bottom of the cart cracking my legs
just above the ankles, "shit," I said
and she backed off and as the long
ash of her cigarette fell to the pavement
she gave me a half-grin, swerved her
rushing chariot around and I knew that
she knew that I knew that one day at one
time her legs her kneecaps her glance her
every word kept men suspended between dream and
reality—that once she knew how to hold a
telephone or fix a braid just so, now,
christ, she banged me
we could have met that night in Atlanta,
Georgia when the wallpaper got as close
as my fingernails
now, she didn't care at all and I cared
a little bit less
stepping inside the automatic doors and
walking toward the line of shopping
carts, I'm sixty, dear, what the
hell.

poets and the foreman

the best of Auden
the best of Jeffers
lines laid down
neatly
dried blood
crisp on the page
in that
cheap room of
peeling wallpaper
and the shadows of
drab men
who had died
there

the best of Auden
the best of Jeffers
you could walk down
the hall to the
crapper
conscious
at least of the
fingernails on
your hands

you could go back
to the bad
wine
and no woman
and not much of a
job in the
morning

the best of Auden
the best of Jeffers
they helped
immensely.

drunk upon
wine and the reading
of them
getting into bed
there
it was steady
it held

as the mice came
out in the dark
and claimed that
in the unknown
city

*

to awaken
having forgotten
the best of Auden and
Jeffers

first the thick bland syrup
on hotcakes
then going in to the
bald fat foreman
with dim eyes
who owned your prong
and your asshole and
your nostril hairs

you remembered and wondered
about Auden and Jeffers
then

the foreman
was a very hard and knowledgeable
guide

he had his own book
you read his
book

and after a while
you got to like him
too

his lines
too
were blood crisp

now I've gotten rid
of Auden and Jeffers and
the foreman

and to be alone
like this
is the way
of course

I really don't miss
the foreman

and there's nothing
left to read
anymore

lately I just read
the daily newspaper
over and over
again

look out across this
place
where some call me
famous
where some call me
a great writer
and I know that nothing
means very much
just as I had suspected
in the
beginning.

for the little one

she's downstairs singing, playing her
guitar, I think she's happier than
usual and I'm glad. sometimes my
mind gets sick and I'm cruel to her.
she weighs one hundred and one
pounds
has small wrists and
her eyes
are often purely sad.

sometimes my needs
make me selfish
a backwash floods my
mind
and I've never been
good
with apology.

I hear her singing
now it's
very late night
and from here
I can see the
lights of the city
and they are sweet as
ripe garden fruits
and this room is
calm
so strange
as if magic had
become normal.

we evolve

at first it seems like fucking is the big thing,
then after that—social consciousness,
then intellectual accomplishment,
and then after that
some fall into religion
others into the arts.
after that begins the gathering of money
and after the gathering of money
the stage where we pretend that
money doesn't matter.
then it's health and hobbies,
travel, and finally just sitting around
thinking vaguely of vague things,
rooting in gardens
hating flies, noise, bad weather, snails,
rudeness, the unexpected, new neighbors,
old friends, drunks, smoking, fucking,
singing, dancing, upstarts,
the postman and weeds.
it gives one the fidgets: waiting on
death.

the man at the piano

the man at the piano
plays a song
he didn't write
sings words
that aren't his
upon a piano
he doesn't own

while
people at tables
eat, drink and talk

the man at the piano
finishes
to no applause

then
begins to play
a new song
he didn't write
begins to sing
words
that aren't his
upon a piano
that isn't his

as the
people at the tables
continue to
eat, drink and talk

when

he finishes
to no applause
he announces
over the mike
that he is
going to take
a ten-minute break

he goes
back to the men's
room
enters
a toilet booth
bolts the door
sits down
pulls out a joint
lights up

he's glad
he's not
at the piano

and the
people at the tables
eating, drinking and talking
are glad
he isn't there
either

this is
the way it goes
almost everywhere
with everybody and
everything
as fiercely
in the highlands

the
black swan burns.

night work

my cat
leaped
into the fireplace
burning
as Van Gogh
slit
the rear screen
and entered
looking
for
the blue whore
of nowhere.

Photo: Michael Montfort